A MAN'S
Guide to
PRAYER

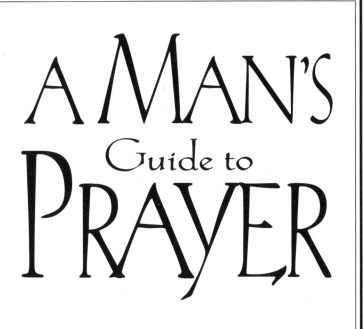

A MAN'S Guide to PRAYER

LINUS MUNDY

A Crossroad Book
The Crossroad Publishing Company
New York

The Crossroad Publishing Company
370 Lexington Avenue, New York, NY 10017

Printed in the United States of America

Library of Congress Cataloging-in-Publication Data

A man's guide to prayer : new ideas, prayers, and meditations from
  many traditions ... / [compiled] by Linus Mundy.
       p.   c.m.
    Includes bibliographical references (p.   ) and index.
    ISBN 0-8245-1762-8
    1. Men – Religious life. 2. Men – Prayer-books and devotions –
English. 3. Prayer – Christianity.   I. Mundy, Linus.
BV4528.2.M3225   1998
248.3'2'081 – dc21   98-7754

1   2   3   4   5   6   7   8   9   10   02   01   00   99   98

To Larry Weber,
a good friend, a good man

Contents

Introduction

This is a book to help men live fully in the present, a book put together by a man like them, one with a particular past. It's a book for men of different faiths, written by one who grew up in a specific faith, just as they did. It's a guide to prayer for men who appreciate their own tradition and other traditions, and who are looking for something a little different.

I grew up, one could say, in an institution of men. It was a place where a thousand men prayed — together and alone. It was a Catholic seminary and monastery, and there I entered at the age of thirteen, studying for the priesthood. For five years there I joined my soul and voice with the male souls and voices of a thousand guys: high school boys, college and school of theology men, and Benedictine monks. I prayed with them, and I prayed alone . . . sometimes very alone — so very alone that I wasn't sure even God was there with me. (As cynic Gertrude Stein might have said of my experience: "Sometimes there wasn't even any *there* there.")

What did I learn in this community of men?

That real men *pray!*

Oh, my dad at home had modeled this for me to some extent, in my childhood, and he especially made it clear to me that "meekness is not weakness" — but he was my dad, for heaven's sake. I needed to see other guys pray — guys who smoked and cussed and hunted and played football, of course, but also guys who read books, liked music, played chess, worked crossword puzzles.

So it was there in the seminary that I learned that praying

wasn't for sissies or guys who couldn't cut it out in the bigger, wider world. Real, normal, all-American boys and men pray. Or they can sure give it a good try.

This is the one important fact I want to share with you in this book for men about prayer: real men pray. But I also want to share with you what I learned, before and after doing seminary time, about male prayer. In writing and preparing to write this book, I've given this theme a good deal of personal reflection, and I've had the privilege of interviewing men from a multitude of faith traditions and a wide range of personal beliefs. So this book won't be just *one* guy's idea of prayer. It will be, I hope, "everyman's."

•

The idea for this book was inspired by a good friend of mine, a writer, who proudly announced to me last winter that she was working on a book about prayer. It is to be a book of Psalm-prayers for women. She was re-writing, just for women, each of the 150 Old Testament Psalms. I was delighted to hear this; and it made me think immediately about doing the converse: Psalm prayers for *men*. After all, the Psalms were *my* prayer; I had discovered them myself — or so I thought — as a high school seminarian, one day in April of 1962. (The discovery was so intense for me that I marked the date in my big black prayer book.) These prayers were *my* prayers, no doubt about it. There I was, a struggling and confused fifteen-year-old boy away from home — looking for a home; I was looking for a *there* there in the seminary — and these prayers pointed the way for me as an adolescent boy. I'd never heard such prayers in my school, or at home where I watched and listened to my dad and big brother pray. I had no idea anyone had the *nerve* to talk to God like that! This Psalm-writer fellow must have been a *real man,* I thought. (And now I know real women pray this way too, and have every right to.)

Some examples of these "tough-language" Psalms: "How long, O Lord? Will you forget me forever? How long will you hide your face from me? How long must I bear pain in my soul, and have sorrow in my heart all day long?" (Ps. 13). "And may he be clothed with cursing as with a robe; may it penetrate into his entrails like water and like oil into his bones" (Ps. 109). These prayers spoke of despair and rage, wars and threats of wars — and skull-bashing. This was good stuff; it was like reading the local sports page about last night's Indiana-Purdue basketball game: "First there was blood, and then there was guts, and then there was hatred.... And then in the second half it got *serious!*"

These Psalms spoke of the loneliness and desolation and singular hardship I knew — the typical inner emotions and experiences of a teenage boy, emotions that were never allowed out in my day (nor so well in our present day, I suppose). How "manly" these prayers were — and are. (Yes, they are "womanly," too. More about this later.) So many of the Psalms refer to battles and wars and labors in the field and at sea and on journeys; and the prayers are about courage and valor and fortitude and strength and righteousness, and on and on. A veritable table of contents for a "Man's Guide to Prayer."

In this guidebook of prayers for men I include a good sampling of these powerfully honest and direct Psalm prayers, as you might expect. But I also include the honest and direct prayers of the men I interviewed and surveyed at quite some length — over a hundred men altogether. These men told me a lot about the present state of the male psyche — and the present state of male prayer.

In Part I of this book I tell you more about these men, and I share their thoughts and ideas about prayer.

In Parts II and III, I share their actual prayers — and mine — as well as prayers by and for men, past and present, from many walks of life and faith. Except where noted, the prayers you'll find in the concluding section — "Original, Contemporary Prayers by and for Men" — have been written by myself, borrowing from many rich sources past and present. It is a privilege to present them in this edition.

About the prayer selections: I intended this book to be both ancient and modern in its offerings, and also to be rather free from distinct themes or categories — or even chronology, for that matter. My hope is that the prayers offered will be seen as time-less. My hope is also that some of them will be seen as downright quirky, because that was surely intended in many cases. This is also a book for men who are looking for something a little different once in a while.

This book recognizes that there is a growing resurgence in our appetite for applying ancient wisdom to our modern times; there is a growing yearning — even among "real men" — to fill the piety void we have felt for a generation or more. Thus the prayers in this book are a broad mix of ancient and new, many of the ancient ones especially chosen to make a point that some of these old-timers speak well to us today.

You will find, then, a full range of prayers and prayer styles and prayer themes. They all show, I think, that things haven't changed much for us over the ages. ("A man prays for toys, just as he did as a boy; it's just that the toys are more expen-sive now.") You will also find a good mix, I hope, of traditional, moderate, and progressive prayers for men, ranging from Chris-tian to Sufi to Native American to Hindu. The prayers in the book come from men of many traditions and from all continents. They are from poets and prophets, novelists and businessmen, saints and sinners. Yes, there is a preponderance of prayers from the Christian tradition, from Jesus to fourth-century St. John Chrysostom, from Benedict to twentieth-century Thomas Mer-ton, for the riches to choose from are great. But there are also more meditative, free-form prayers from widely diverse sources to serve as "prayer-starters" to inspire your own prayer.

The prayers in this book are especially chosen, written, and prayed in many cases first and foremost by and for men. This is not to imply that they are exclusively "male prayers," however. Yes, this book is intended as a book for men. But it is certainly not the private domain of the male gender to possess the many "characteristics" attributed rather blatantly to men in some of these prayers. Far from it! Indeed, a great many prayers in this volume have nothing whatsoever to do with the reader's (pray-er's) gender. But they were chosen or composed with the benefit of the male reader in mind.

It is my hope that after you've finished this book the first time through you will go back to certain passages and prayers and visit them in prayer. Like St. Paul, let us be mindful of the following: "Whatever is true, whatever is honorable, whatever is right, whatever is pure, whatever is lovely, whatever is of good repute, if there is any excellence and if anything worthy of praise, let your mind dwell on these things" (Phil. 4:8).

The reader will see that free use has been made of numerous sources in an effort to offer a wide variety of viewpoints and "theologies." I also made a sincere effort to offer prayers for and about men of all levels of prayer "indoctrination" — or non-indoctrination. One will need little background in prayer, meditation, theology, or spirituality, to profit from reading many of the prayers, I assure you. A little learning is not a dangerous thing in this case — for we are all learning, even we who were trained-up in prayer at formal institutions. We need not worry about "drinking deep . . . or tasting not," as Tennyson put it. Even the smallest taste of prayer that speaks to our minds and hearts and souls — really speaks — will be a "deep drink."

At the end of this work is a bibliography of sources cited; it also offers some fine book selections to inspire and guide men further into this marvelous thing we call prayer. Also included is a subject index so you can go there first to find just what you need to pray right now. The purpose of the *Man's Guide to Prayer* is to help us live fully in the present.

PART I

How Men Pray — and How Their Prayer Is Different

How many of these adjectives can you relate to?

___ Industrious	___ Organized
___ Left-brained	___ Mechanical
___ Practical	___ Rational
___ Businesslike	___ Productive
___ Efficient	___ Results-oriented
___ Impersonal	___ Abrupt
___ Controlling	___ Strong

Well, my *grandmother* was all of these; and my wife and daughter and sisters are no slouches when it comes to any of these traits either. So please understand this book is not about establishing — or perpetuating — stereotypes. It is about recognizing that men's and women's prayer styles can be very different, and that there is some validity to the phrase: "To each his (or her) own."

No, I'm not one who thinks there are no differences between men and women in their psychological make-up. There clearly are differences, and we need to appreciate them. For example, my experience leads me to believe that men are more prone to being self-centered than women, that in general men operate out of calculative tendencies, that men can be rightly accused of abusing power, that men's egos are more easily threatened than women's. Indeed, some days I find myself in agreement with writer Paul Theroux, who once said: "I have always disliked being a man. . . . Even the expression 'Be a man!' strikes me as insulting and abusive. It means: Be stupid, be unfeeling, obedient and soldierly, and stop thinking. Manliness . . . is a hideous and crippling lie, . . . it is also by its very nature destructive — emotionally damaging and socially harmful." But more often, I find myself agreeing with one of my wise male friends whom I asked to contribute a "male" prayer to this book. His reply was: "Generally I find gender comparisons odious."

"Repulsive" is another word that on occasion might apply to the exercise. That's a word one of my favorite writers, Stephen Jay Gould, used when critiquing a philosophical primer on the subject of gender differences. Gould refers to a book by Edmund Burke first published in 1756: *A Philosophical Inquiry into the Origin of Our Ideas of the Sublime and the Beautiful.* By the "sublime" and the "beautiful" Burke is referring to the male and the female. He argues, in essence (and in excess), that it is in the male's distinct nature to be "a configuration of the sublime" — with the sublime, or "great," being based on the male's instinct toward *self-preservation — founded in terror.* Burke then lists some adjunct "male" attributes: vastness, darkness, roughness, solidity, massiveness, infinity.

The female, on the other hand (says Burke), is "aligned with the configuration of the beautiful" — with tendencies rooted in pleasure and linked to the instinct for generation "necessary for the preservation of our race." Burke lists for the female such attributes as smallness, smoothness, delicacy, transparency, lack of ambiguity, weakness, and bright colors. And to raise eyebrows even further, I quote: "The sublime . . . always dwells on great objects, and terrible; [beauty] on small ones, and pleasing. . . . The beauty of women is considerably owing to their weakness or delicacy, and is even enhanced by their timidity, a quality of mind analogous to it."

Pretty "odious" and "repulsive," isn't it? And yet what is truly odious and repulsive is that in some ways we are still not much more enlightened than Burke when he drew the above conclusions in 1756.

There *are* differences, of course, between male and female. And folks everywhere seem to be interested in examining these differences at length, perhaps thereby "Improving Communication and Getting What You Want in Your Relationship," to quote the sub-title of the best-selling *Men Are from Mars, Women Are from Venus*.

One way that men and women today are said to be different is in their ethical behavior. Indeed, more men than women appear to be recognized as sinners. A recent Religion News Service poll (copyright RNS, 1997, conducted by Paquette and Sappington) asked 1,003 adults: "Do you think that women or men are more ethical in their behavior?" Fifty-one percent responded Women; 25 percent responded Equally Ethical; 10 percent responded Men; and 13 percent responded Not Sure. But this book is not about male-bashing nor is it about female-bashing. (Writer Frederic Hayward, in his book *To Be a Man*, recounts how two authors told him about pressure from their editors to create anti-male titles as a way of increasing sales. But the closest thing to a female flaw that one can publicly acknowledge today is that women tend to "love too much." Hayward goes on to describe the popular anti-male products now available. A couple of examples include the 3-M Post-It Notes that say things like: "The more I know about men, the more I like my dog," and "There are only two things wrong with men . . . everything they say and everything they do.")

And then there are our commonalities. Even at the tender age of ten, in the glorious and innocent 1950s, I could see that the really big challenges in life men and women had in common. I remember telling my cousin Jim my succinct and much-distilled insight about all this: "It doesn't matter if you're a girl or a boy; we're stuck either way: boys grow up and need to become soldiers; girls grow up and need to have babies!" Or it might be put like this: "People [not men or women] have it tougher than anybody." As Joan Baez said in a November 1997 *Rolling Stone* interview: "I see the whole human race as being broken and terribly in need, not just women [or men]."

Challenges in life — serious ones — will always be there for us, whether we are girl or boy, man or woman. But so will serious opportunities. And this book is about some of the serious opportunities men have to pray, and to pray more sublimely and more beautifully than they have ever imagined.

All of us, men and women alike, have much to learn from each other about life — and about prayer. We men are learning that women survive better than we do because their feelings and emotions get expressed. And some of us men are looking at other, more "enlightened" men, men with perhaps a better balance of *animus* and *anima,* and wondering why we can't think and act and feel and pray a bit more like them — men who seem to recognize that our feelings and emotions, too, can help us find meaning. Indeed these feelings and emotions can take us places where thinking alone simply cannot penetrate. In a world structured greatly around logic and analytical thinking, we men can feel our way through to some whole new areas. And prayer can help us toward "right feeling." Prayer has always been a basic practice for breaking new ground. Plato wrote to Socrates that "all men, Socrates, who have any degree of right feeling, at the beginning of every enterprise, whether small or great, always call upon God."

Prayer is about relationships; it's about intimacy. Yet no matter how much we may yearn to grow closer to God, there is a part of us that wants to remain cool and aloof. As one husband said to his wife, who complained of his absence of expressed affection: "Honey, I told you when I married you that I loved you; can't you just believe that until I tell you otherwise?" It's a human thing, I suppose, and it's clearly a male thing, to take the "cool and detached" posture. The "strong, silent type" has become more than a cliché. Our very image of God may be a similar one: We see God as someone who loves us — until we hear otherwise.

Likewise, for God to get a prayer out of some of us not-so-expressive men is like the reporter who tried to get something out of President Calvin Coolidge. A friend bet the reporter she wouldn't get three words out of him. The reporter went in and Coolidge only pointed to the door, saying: "You lose."

We men lose by not giving more than two or three words to our God who wants to speak with us. What we need to do — according to the modern lingo — is "mancipate" ourselves; that is, we need to liberate ourselves from being distant, disconnected, super-analytical — especially in our relationship with God. We can take John Bunyan's observation only so far: "In prayer it is better to have a heart without words than words without a heart." True. But what about having a heart *and* some words? Yes, that goes for us German types especially, who like Martin Luther would say: "The fewer the words, the better the prayer."

•

So how are men to pray? And what is prayer anyway? To begin to find out, I sent out a written questionnaire to over a hundred men: friends and strangers, young and old, men of many faiths and of no professed faith. I asked them to respond in writing to a few specific questions. Here are the questions — and the answers they gave me. I follow each with some commentary.

1. I would best describe or define prayer as:

53% Communicating with God

21% Talking to God

9% Giving thanks to God

9% Praising God

6% Listening to God

2% Other (e.g., awareness of God's presence)

0% Expressing needs to God

With "Communicating with God" as the clear winner here, it seems to be readily recognized that prayer is about relationship: our relationship and connectedness with God. How are we men at relationships? Are we attentive? Devoted? Adoring? Do we apologize after mistakes? Do we readily forgive? Do we talk? Do we want to be together? Respondent Matthew Kelty, a sprightly Trappist monk who is now eighty-something, takes the position that silence in a relationship can be golden. He describes the perfect loving relationship by saying: "The silent, wordless love of an old couple together by the fire is the best picture of the love of God I know." Others take an opposite or "balanced" view.

Do we listen? "Half of prayer is listening," one male friend reminded me. Or, as Simon Tugwell puts it: "So long as we imagine it is we who have to look for God, we must often lose heart. But it is the other way around: God is looking for us, and God will not give up."

"I'd like to spend more time in silence and be comfortable with it," wrote one man. This whole idea of contemplative prayer for men came up here. In a society that stresses so much the male ideals of action, accomplishment and performance, we need to perform a real balancing act of "Do-Be Do-Be-Do"! Writing in the journal *Spiritual Life*, Patrick and Claudette McDonald ("God

Is There All the Time, And Now We Can Name It," Winter 1997), the authors declare that "mysticism" and its sister word "contemplation" are the most misunderstood words in the religious vocabulary. "Suspiciousness of the word flows from some assumptions that seem common to married couples: that contemplation is the domain of professional religious, or open only to elite who are trained in theology. Some associate it with a celibate life or reserve it for those who have labored through the stages of the ascetic way. Others restrict it to a monastic setting, seeing it as territory to those who possess a higher calling."

"It's okay that you don't even know what contemplative prayer is," commented one person. "If I just do what I think contemplative prayer is, it will be good enough for God — and good enough for me."

Wrote in another survey respondent: "Prayer is a two-way exchange — although sometimes I talk too much and have to say to myself, 'Good grief, will you shut up!'"

Another man described prayer as "a longing for God — an attempt to line up with God and having God's perspective on things." And this from a respondent who declared he prayed rarely: "Prayer means acknowledging spiritual guidance from God as well as acknowledging God's having granted us the strength to overcome challenges in this world."

2. I pray:

71% Daily

17% For special needs/on special occasions

6% Weekly

6% Rarely

Even though a large majority of respondents said they prayed daily, 6 percent did admit that they prayed rarely. One man even added the word "Very" in front of rarely. My survey included a good number of male friends whom I know are interested in prayer and religion. But I suspect that the answers had to do with each person's definition of prayer. "I pray while I shave," wrote in one respondent, "having said my morning prayers before getting out of bed." But no matter how we interpret prayer, some men (and women) just don't get around to it. And they admit to it.

3. I pray most often:

23% To give thanks

23% For family

17% To praise God

8% For work

7% For the world

6% For dying

5% For peace

4% For good health

7% For sports victories

6% Other (e.g, forgiveness, friends, people in need)

"Far more important than how I pray is why I pray," wrote one respondent. "I pray for wisdom," responded one man; "Friends," answered another. "The intentions that others have asked me to pray for," wrote in another.

"I pray that I will change," wrote another. "If we change ourselves, and that is all we are capable of, the world will be a better place." Another responded tenderly: "I pray for guidance from my angel, my deceased grandmother."

"Pray for sports victories? Never!" emphatically stated one man. (Oh, for a national survey on this one!)

4. I pray:

58% Alone

22% With my church group

8% With my spouse

8% With other family members

4% Other (e.g., Bible group, community, friends, groups)

"We need to realize we don't go it alone," commented one survey respondent. "That's the bottom line, whatever the problem, whatever the challenge. We're in good hands." "The work's already been done," said another. "We don't have to do a thing — we're saved! Why can't we accept that?"

5. I pray:

40% At home

29% At church

21% At work

5% At school

5% Other (e.g, in the car, walking, in bed, "wherever I am")

Commented one respondent: "I pray in the car; while exercising on a treadmill; while hiking in the woods." Said another: "I talk to God while I'm driving." "Usually it's very early in the morning, while I'm still in bed," responded another. "Going to and from work are my best times," wrote in another man.

"Sitting near a stream or waterfall is a very good way for me to feel in touch with God," writes Harry Faulkner, of Evansville, Indiana. "Sometimes as I meditate I use a mantra: 'I have the light within me.'"

"I like to pray in the woods," writes my Trappist monk-friend, Matthew Kelty. And at Communion I pray: 'Come into the shambles of my heart, dearest Lord; come into the shanty I call home.'"

Not a survey respondent, but a man with much spiritual insight to share, is writer Frederick Buechner. "I pray all the time at odd moments," says Buechner in *Sacred Journey* (November 1997), "like driving somewhere in the car, or waiting for something to happen like sleep, or being for some reason or another particularly sad, or scared, or happy, or you name it. They are mostly very brief, rather fragmented prayers, but there is one formal one, known sometimes as St. Patrick's Breastplate, that is currently full of power for me. It begins: 'Christ be with me, Christ within me, Christ behind me, Christ beside me, Christ to win me, Christ to comfort and restore me."

And when does Buechner find God speaking back? "If skeptics ask to be shown an instance of God speaking to them in their lives, I suggest they pay closest attention to the next time when, for unaccountable reasons, they find tears in their eyes."

6. I pray:

47% Using my own words

29% Using words from my own faith tradition

22% With no words

2% Other

Both formal and informal prayer came in strong here. Wrote one respondent: "I like to keep it loose, free-style, so I can say to God things like, 'Hey, look at this, God. What are we going to do about this?'" Citing the more formal approach, one Catholic commented: "I pray the Psalms and prayers from the liturgy — especially the opening prayers at Mass." "I pray the Office of Readings each morning," a monk-friend told me, "including petitions in my own words, and then I try to just sit in silence for a while."

7. My prayer is "inspired" by:

25% Needs I see

20% My own needs

14% Nature

13% God

13% Books I read (Scripture, sacred texts)

12% People I know

 3% My minister/priest/rabbi/spiritual leader

In an October 1997 survey in *US Catholic,* 69 percent of respondents agreed with the statement: "It is good for Christians to learn from and adopt non-Christian spiritual traditions." And the Christian men I surveyed seemed to support this finding.

"Short cries from the heart, taken from Scripture, really work for me," wrote one respondent. "Open my heart, Lord." "That I may see." "Grant me patience, Lord."

When we talk about our prayer being "inspired by" something, we are talking about the "feelings." Evelyn Underhill reminds us in her *Letters:* "Don't be disappointed that you don't *feel* anything [in your prayer]; this does not affect the main point, which is that our Lord comes to your soul to *feed* you, not to give you sensations, and you come to offer Him your whole self, not just your emotional life.... Faithfulness is the main thing asked of us — and however imperfect our dispositions, that does not diminish the fullness and the beauty of the divine gift, or the reality of the Presence which is there just the same, whether we feel it or not."

Underhill refers to Teresa of Avila's similar admonition to us pray-ers, male and female alike: "The love of God does not consist in tears or in this delight or tenderness [in prayer], which for the greater part we desire and find consolation in; but it consists in serving with justice and fortitude of soul and in humility."

One man, responding to the survey question about what inspired his prayer, responded simply: "Most people need more specific instruction on prayer — when and how to pray, etc."

8. I am:

57% Satisfied with my prayer life.

43% Not satisfied with my prayer life.

"Do you know anybody that is?" asked one respondent, somewhat miffed by the question.

Wrote one respondent: "I'm satisfied, because I know it will always be changing." Also: "I believe that people's personality determines their prayer life mostly, though I suppose that socialization as men, women, etc., plays a part."

"I'm satisfied," wrote one respondent, "because I am praying; I'm not satisfied because I still want to grow in the spirit of prayer."

9. Men pray differently than women:

79% Agree

21% Disagree

One of the respondents wrote: "I think that probably most men feel comfortable with a different type of prayer-language than women." One astute social worker summed it up: "There's only one thing we need to believe to have the healing presence of the love of God in your life — whether you're a man or a woman, young or old, black or white — and that is: You gotta realize that You're Not It; GOD is It. When I realize this, this puts me into right relationship with God."

Wrote another: "I'm not sure that men and women pray differently because they are of different sexes. I think that we all pray differently because we are different individuals."

"I think women are far ahead of men in integrating the masculine and feminine parts of themselves," responded one man.

"Why are most men so reluctant to pray out loud?" queried one man. And another man asked: "Why are men afraid to pray? Is it a control issue?"

Another categorized things this way: "I think we men think more community-minded as a rule, and women are more home-minded as a rule."

"I heard on a mini-series on male spirituality," wrote in one man, "that the general difference between male and female spirituality is that — generally speaking — women accept/receive the mystery of God's presence in their lives . . . and men want to pierce/understand the mystery of God. This difference has held up in conversations I've had with both men and women."

"I'm really not certain there is a distinction between the male spirit and the female spirit, except in our perceptions of the two," commented one man.

Another respondent summed it up this way: "I feel that most men, while it is less apparent outwardly, have just as intense a communication with God as women, who are more obvious in their devotion."

10. I believe, in general, that compared to women men pray differently in the following way:

26% For different purposes

24% Less

13% With less emotion

12% Shorter

11% With more expectation of "results"

3% With more originality

3% With less expectation of "results"

2% With less originality

2% Longer

2% With more emotion

2% Other (e.g., With less formality)

0% More

While a great many respondents wrote comments like: "I never thought about this" or "I'm not in a position to judge this" or "I have no idea," others made fairly specific comments.

"Most of us guys need to write a book about ourselves called *Sorry, I'm Not the Messiah* . . . and then also do a sequel called *I'm Not Even Close!* We really struggle with power and control issues, I know, and we need to turn these over to God."

Another respondent pointed to a book called *Driven by Hope: Men and Meaning* (by James E. Dittes, Westminster, 1996) which challenges recent assessments that condemn men as driven, controlling, withholding. For the author, men are instead "inherently religious, afflicted and impelled by a relentless expectancy that life is created to be more whole and holy than we now know." Men are chronically destined to yearn for all that God has in store. A man's "drivenness" may be seen as commitment, his "controlling" may be reframed as solicitous caring, his "withholding" as profoundly spiritual caution about affording undue allegiance to unworthy objects.

The cardinal rule of manhood, recently commented news reporter Mike Wallace, is this: whatever afflicts you, just suck it up and go. "I just don't want to talk about it" is the motto. "We can't treat God and prayer that way," one survey respondent emphasized. "God never asked any of us to take on the world by ourselves!"

Wrote another, "We men are sometimes too proud to plead — maybe especially when things are going well." Utter dependence on God seems not very American and certainly not very "manly."

In this regard Abraham Lincoln cautions us: "Intoxicated with unbroken successes, we have become too self-sufficient to feel the necessity of redeeming and preserving grace, too proud to pray to the God that made us." Lincoln realized that it was time to pray.

In *What Are They Saying about Masculine Spirituality?* (Paulist, 1997) David C. James says that a man's ability or inability to establish authentic friendships and support systems influences his lifetime search for meaning and God. Because men alienate themselves from one another and compete with one another at break-neck pace, certain compulsions set in, says James: "Given men's inability to form authentic relationships, it is not surprising to discover that they look to others to provide them with feelings of acceptance, passion and significance.... Men have been socialized to view sexual activity as the chief means of receiving intimacy and tenderness."

"I believe that all of us pray differently," commented one survey respondent. "We are all individuals and our life experiences lead us to how we pray and throughout our lives we will all change — due to our experiences — and thus our prayer life should change and grow."

•

I also asked the respondents: "What is your favorite prayer?" The Lord's Prayer was most often mentioned, followed by the Jesus Prayer (see p. 71), the Prayer of Thomas Merton (see p. 135), the Psalms, the Serenity Prayer (see p. 146), and the Peace Prayer of St. Francis.

It is no surprise that so many respondents chose the Psalms as a favorite prayer. The Book of Psalms is Israel's prayer book — and ours. The prayers are so bluntly honest that they shock us: Psalm 137 even asks God to smash the heads of our enemies' babies!

The others mentioned are familiar prayers frequently seen on "prayer cards" or plaques and often prayed in unison at church or at support group meetings of various types.

"My favorite prayer? The Our Father — also known as 'The Lord's Prayer' — but prayed very slowly," says one of the survey respondents, my friend Dr. Richard Stern.

"Many mornings," wrote respondent Charles Roth, from Manhasset, New York, "I look at a picture of my father, taken when he was about thirty years old (I was three or four). He looks wonderful — in the full vigor of manhood. I feel how much I love him and I pray the Opening Prayer for Tuesday, the Sixth Week of Easter: God, Our Father, may we look forward with hope to our resurrection, for you have made us your sons and daughters, and restored the joy of our youth."

"My favorite prayer," writes Tom McGrath of Chicago, "is simply: 'God help.'" And wrote Al Cassidy of Louisville, Kentucky: "Please help our children and grandchildren know the will of God...and follow it."

"I must decrease; He must increase," is the favorite prayer of Dave Schimmell, a firefighter from Evansville, Indiana, who continues: "My prayers are always different, but I basically pray for the same thing: 'Help me to not think of myself as so goshdarn important. I know in my life that *me* is the main God that I worship and serve and it tortures me that I am that way. Help me to turn over my controls to you and live in the total peace of your care and wise guidance, not concerned with results, not concerned with how things affect me so much as how I can do something 'for the good of the whole.' Let that be my desire and not so much my self."

"My prayers have three sections," writes Fred Smith of Bloomington, Indiana. "(1) Thanks to God for my family and asking for help over rough spots; (2) Thanks for those who have died: family, relatives, colleagues, friends; (3) Prayer for the living who have problems — health, social, financial. I also pray sometimes when I can't sleep — I may pray for an hour or so."

"My daily prayer is trusting faith in God's grace and power to prevent illness and bad things," writes Gerard Malloy of Port Washington, New York. My favorite prayer is what I call "Pleading the Blood of Jesus" — recalling each instance of his passion: blood shedding, gathering it (spiritually) and washing/staining myself and all who come to mind each day with that once-shed blood. It washes away all stain of sin, and washes our spiritual garments white as snow. It stains white; it defeats Satan." Here is a prayer composed by Malloy, based on Ephesians 3:16:

> Father, out of your infinite glory and riches give us the power through your Spirit for our hidden inner selves to grow strong — so strong that Christ may live in our hearts through faith; and then, planted in love and built in love, we will with all the saints have strength to grasp the love of Christ — its width and length, its height and depth, until knowing this love of Christ which is beyond all knowledge, we are filled with your utter fullness. Glory be to you, Father, your power working in us can do infinitely more than we can ask or imagine. Glory be to you from generation to generation in the church and in Christ Jesus for ever and ever.

"Praying *for* something is a misunderstanding of what God is," writes my friend Don Aronoff, of Santa Claus, Indiana, who was brought up in the Jewish tradition. "God is the word we use for all majesty and the mystery of the universe — and you don't ask this Awesomeness for stuff!"

As for my own "favorite" prayers, I am amused by the irreverent prayer in the *Hebrew Authorized Daily Prayer Book*, and included here (see p. 101 below) primarily to show the wide range of "male" prayers: "I thank God that thou has not made me a woman." (This sounds like the modern prayer of a movie character played by actor Jack Nicholson!) I'm also quite fond of the 1666 diary entry of Samuel Pepys: "I bless God that I am worth more than ever yet I was, which is 6,200 pounds, for which the Holy Name of God be praised!" (see p. 102). I also like this simple, unabashed prayer composed by Edward Caswall, in his *Lyra Catholica,* 1849: "My God, I love Thee; not because I hope for heaven thereby" (see p. 87).

And I also include the long St. Benedict Prayer (see below, p. 111). It is nothing less than a creed to live by, emphasizing the need for balance in our lives. And that means balance in all things — which I think is especially pertinent to any discussion of male-female differences and attitudes, traits, and attributes. But perhaps the greatest prayer-line of all in this book comes from Trappist monk Thomas Merton: "...The fact that I think I am following your will does not mean that I am actually doing so. But I believe that the desire to please you does in fact please you." (see p. 135 for the complete prayer). Merton also said: "How do I pray? I breathe!"

PART II

Favorite Prayers for Men — from Many Traditions

It can be frustrating to realize that many of the problems we face in today's world have been problems throughout the ages. But it also gives us consolation to find that in Aristotle's or St. Benedict's or Chief Joseph's day, too, not even a philosopher could tolerate a toothache very philosophically.

No matter the time or the culture, those who have gone before us felt the universal longing to voice their praises, their convictions — and their bewilderment — to their God.

This section of *A Man's Guide to Prayer* contains the prayers of many "philosophers" — with and without toothaches. It also contains the prayers of everyday folks like us who know life's incredible sorrows and joys and in-betweens.

May we draw from this rich devotional heritage as we speak in our own time and culture to our own God.

1. From Me to Thee

Lord, hear me out,
and hear me out this day:
From me to Thee's
a long and terrible way.

— THEODORE ROETHKE

2. You Know Me Best, Lord

I thank you, Lord, for knowing me better than I know
myself,
And for letting me know myself better than others
know me.
Make me, I pray to you, better than they suppose,
And forgive me for what they do not know.

— ABU BAKR, the first Caliph of Islam

3. Not All Brains

Help me to see that although
I am in the wilderness
it is not all brains and barrenness.
I have — bread from heaven,
streams from the rock,
light by day, fire by night,
thy dwelling place and thy mercy seat.

I am sometimes discouraged by the way,
but though winding and trying,
it is safe and short.

> — Puritan prayer

4. Past, Present, Future

My Past, O Lord,
To Your Mercy,
My Present, O Lord,
To Your Love,
My Future, O Lord,
To Your Providence.

> — PADRE PIO

5. O Thou of Wide Fame

Like father to a son, most kind, O Soma;
Thoughtful like friend to friend,
O thou of wide fame.

> — *Rig Veda*, VIII, 48, 4

6. A "Macho" Prayer

Let the waves roar,
Let the wind blow,
Let the world turn
upside down.
Let everything be in darkness,
in smoke, in uproar.
Nothing can hurt me.
God is near.

> — ST. FRANCIS DE SALES

7. Useless

O Lord, let us not live to be useless;
for Christ's sake.
Amen.

— JOHN WESLEY

8. To Rest in Thee

Thou hast made us for thyself,
And our heart is restless until it rests in thee.

— ST. AUGUSTINE

9. May All Be Well

May it be beautiful, my fire;
May it be delightful for my children;
May all be well.
May it be delightful with my food and theirs.
May all my possessions be well,
and may they be made to increase.

— Navajo prayer

10. Prayer of an Unknown Confederate Soldier

I asked for strength that I might achieve;
I was made weak that I might learn humbly to obey.
I asked for health that I might do greater things;
I was given infirmity that I might do better things.
I asked for riches that I might be happy;
I was given poverty that I might be wise.
I asked for power that I might have the praise of men;
I was given weakness that I might feel the need of God.

I asked for all things that I might enjoy life;
I was given life that I might enjoy all things.
I got nothing that I had asked for,
but everything that I had hoped for.
Almost despite myself my unspoken prayers were answered;
I am, among all men, most richly blessed.

11. Prayer of Thanks

Deo gratias.
Thanks be to God.

12. Walk in Beauty

In beauty may I walk.
Soft goods may I acquire.
Hard goods may I acquire.
Horses may I acquire.
Sheep may I acquire.

In old age wandering.
Trail beautiful.
Lively may I walk.

— Navajo prayer

13. Part of Us

Thou art part and parcel of all things equally, O Creator:
Thou must feel for all men and all nations.

— Hymns of GURU NANAK, *Khurasan*

14. Be Like You

"I wanna be like ... Jesus."

15. Give Me Work

God give me work
Till my life shall end
And life
Till my work is done.

— Epitaph of WINIFRED HOLTBY

16. The Benedictus

*Zechariah was made dumb because of his doubts in God's ability
to make him a father at such an advanced aged. When the child
was finally born, they were going to call the child Zechariah
after his father, but his mother said in reply, "No, he will be
called John." They answered her: "But there is no one by that
name among your relatives." So they made signs and asked the
father what to do. He asked for a tablet and wrote: "His name
shall be John." And from that moment his mouth was opened,
his tongue freed, and he spoke, blessing God as follows:*

Blessed be the Lord, the God of Israel,
for he has visited and brought redemption to his people.
He has raised up a horn for our salvation
within the house of David his servant,
even as he promised through the mouth of his holy
    prophets from of old:
salvation from our enemies
and from the hand of all who hate us,
to show mercy to our fathers
and to be mindful of his holy covenant
and of the oath he swore to Abraham our father,
and to grant us that, rescued from the hand of enemies,
without fear we might worship him
in holiness and righteousness

before him all our days.
And you, child, will be called
prophet of the Most High,
for you will go before the Lord to prepare his ways,
to give his people knowledge of salvation
through the forgiveness of their sins,
because of the tender mercy of our God
by which the daybreak from on high will visit us
to shine on those who sit in darkness and death's shadow,
to guide our feet into the path of peace.

— Luke 1:68–79

17. Prayer Near Death

Jesus, help me to overcome when the final struggle begins.
Stand by me and give me the victory.
Help me in my distress and weakness.
Let your grace strengthen me.
After the fight, the crown; after the battle, the victory!
How gloriously I will be adorned and crowned by you after
   my death.
Show me the crown which you have prepared for me,
and fill my soul with your gracious presence.

— *Be with Me*

18. Pure Love

Jesus, thou art all compassion,
Pure abounded love thou art;
Visit us with thy salvation,
Enter every trembling heart.

— CHARLES WESLEY

19. O God, Our Help in Ages Past

O God, our help in ages past,
Our hope for years to come,
Be thou our guard while troubles last,
And our eternal home.

— Isaac Watts

20. Hear Me

Hear me, O Lord,
for Your loving kindness is good....

— Psalm 69:16

21. Prayer for Trust

Help me, O Lord,
to throw myself absolutely and wholly on thee,
for better, for worse,
without comfort, and all but hopeless.

— Puritan prayer

22. As a Child

Give me a mountaintop
as high as the valley is low.
All-wise God,
your never-failing providence
orders every event,
sweetens every fear....
Out of my sorrow and night...
help me to love as your child.

— Puritan prayer

23. House Blessing

God bless the house
From site to stay,
From beam to wall,
From end to end,
From ridge to basement,
From balk to roof-tree,
From found to summit,
Found and summit.

— Celtic prayer

24. Prayer for Entering a New House

My father built,
And his father built,
And I have built.
Leave me to live here in success,
Let me sleep in comfort,
And have children.
There is food for you.

— A prayer from Uganda

25. May We Be the Ones

May we be the ones
whom your thoughts will embrace.
For this, on this day
to our sun father,
we offer prayer meal.
To this end:
May you help us all to finish our roads.

— Zuni prayer

26. For a Fiancée

That I may come near to her,
draw me nearer to thee than to her;
that I may know her,
make me to know thee more than her;
that I may love her with the perfect love
of a perfectly whole heart,
cause me to love thee more than her and most of all.
Amen. Amen.

That nothing may come between me and her,
be thou between us, every moment.
That we may be constantly together,
draw us into separate loneliness with thyself.
And when we meet breast to breast, my God,
let it be on thine own.
Amen. Amen.

— TEMPLE GAIRDNER OF CAIRO

27. For Results

Lord, give me the grace to bring about
the things that I pray for.

— ST. THOMAS MORE

28. Prayer of Protection

The light of God surrounds me;
The love of God enfolds me;
The power of God protects me;
The presence of God watches over me.
Whatever I am, God is.

— Anonymous

29. Strike the Chords

I shall sing a praise to God:
Strike the chords upon the drum.
God who gives us all good things —
Strike the chords upon the drum —
Wives, and wealth, and wisdom.
Strike the chords upon the drum.

— A prayer from Zaire

30. Singing Praises

We will sing thy praises,
O God almighty.
We will now and evermore
sing thy praises,
even as they were sung of old.
For thy laws are immutable, O God:
they are firm like the mountains.

— The Vedas

31. Jesus' Final Prayer

Father,
Into your hands
I commend
My spirit.

— Luke 23:46

32. Partners

You are the notes, and we are the flute.
We are the mountain, you are the sounds coming down.

We are the pawns and kings and rooks
you set out on a board: we win or we lose.
We are lions rolling and unrolling on flags.
Your invisible wind carries us through the world.

—JELALUDDIN RUMI

33. Hasidic Song

Wherever I go — only Thou!
Wherever I stand — only Thou!
Just Thou, again Thou!
always Thou! Thou, Thou,
Thou! When things are good,
Thou! when things are bad —
Thou! Thou, Thou, Thou!

34. Batter My Heart

Batter my heart, three-person'd God, for you
As yet but knock! Breathe, shine, and seek to mend; . . .

Yet dearly I love you, and would be loved fain,
But am betrothed unto your enemy.
Divorce me, untie, or break that knot again;
Take me to you, imprison me, for I,
Except you enthrall me, never shall be free,
Nor ever chaste, except you ravish me.

—JOHN DONNE

35. I'm Stupid, Lord

Lord, I am blind and helpless, stupid and ignorant,
Cause me to hear;

cause me to know;
Teach me to do; lead me.

— HENRY MARTYN

36. Opening Prayer

In the Name of God,
the merciful Lord of mercy.
Praise be to God, the Lord of all being,
the merciful Lord of mercy,
Master of the day of judgment.
You alone we serve:
to You alone we come for aid.
Guide us in the straight path,
the path of those whom You have blessed,
not of those against whom there is displeasure,
nor of those who go astray.

— The Koran

37. I Am the Cause

Remember, merciful Jesu,
That I am the cause of your journey.

— WOLFGANG AMADEUS MOZART, *Requiem*

38. An East African Canticle

All you big things, bless the Lord.
Mount Kilimanjaro and Lake Victoria,
The Rift Valley and the Serengeti Plain,
Fat baobabs and shady mango trees,
All eucalyptus and tamarind trees,
Bless the Lord.

Praise and extol Him forever and ever.
All you tiny things, bless the Lord.
Busy black ants and hopping fleas,
Wriggling tadpoles and mosquito larvae,
Flying locusts and water drops,
Pollen dust and tsetse flies,
Millet seed and dried dagaa,
Bless the Lord.
Praise and extol Him forever and ever.

39. As Little as My Bed

Teach me to live that I may dread
The grave as little as my bed;
Teach me to die so I may
Rise glorious at that awesome day.

— THOMAS KEN

40. Canticle of Simeon

Now, master, you can allow your servant
To depart in peace;
for you have fulfilled your word.
My eyes have witnessed your salvation
displayed for all the peoples to see:
a light of revelation for the Gentiles
and the glory of your people Israel.

— Luke 2:29–32

41. Prayer for Gentleness

Lord of the loving heart, may mine be loving too,
Lord of the gentle hands, may mine be gentle too.

Lord of the willing feet, may mine be willing too,
So I may grow more like thee
In all I say and do.

— Author unknown

42. Traditional Cry for Help

O God, come to my assistance.
O Lord, make haste to help me!

43. The Beautiful Trail

With your feet I walk.
I walk with your limbs.
I carry forth your body.
For me your mind thinks.
Your voice speaks for me.
Beauty is before me.
And beauty is behind me.
Above and below me hovers the beautiful.
I am surrounded by it.
I am immersed in it.
In my youth I am aware of it.
And in old age I shall walk quietly.
The beautiful trail.

— Navajo prayer

44. A Sufi Prayer

My praise dispraises Thee,
Almighty God,
for praise is being
and to be is sin.

45. The Universal Prayer

Teach me to feel another's woe,
To hide the fault I see;
That mercy I to others show,
That mercy show to me.

— ALEXANDER POPE

46. I Set My Soul in Peace

O Lord, my heart is not proud
Nor haughty my eyes.
I have not gone after things too great
Nor marvels beyond me.
Truly I have set my soul
In silence and peace.
O Israel, hope in the Lord,
Both now and forever.

— Psalm 42

47. A West African Prayer

Lord, we brought in the harvest.
The rain watered the earth,
the sun drew cassava and corn out of the clay.
Your mercy showered blessing after
blessing over our country.
Creeks grew into rivers; swamps became lakes.
Healthy fat cows gaze on the green sea of the savanna.
The rain smoothed out the clay walls,
the mosquitoes drowned in the high waters.
Lord, the yam is fat like meat,
the cassava melts on the tongue,
oranges burst in their peels, dazzling and bright.

Lord, nature gives thanks,
Your creatures give thanks.
Your praise rises in us like a great river.

48. The One

He who is in the sun,
and in the fire and in the heart of man is ONE.
He who knows this is one with the ONE.

— The Upanishads

49. Save My Feet

My heart lies before you, O Lord my God.
Look deep within.
See these memories of mine,
for you are my hope.
You cleanse me
when unclean humors such as these possess me,
by drawing my eyes to yourself
and saving my feet from the snare.

— St. Augustine

50. Sabbath Morning Prayer

As it is written:
All my bones shall say,
"Lord, who is like You?
You save the poor from one stronger then he,
the poor and needy from his despoiler."

— Psalm 35:10

51. Conclusion of the "Shemoneh Esrei"

May the word of my mouth
and the meditation of my heart
be acceptable to Thee, O Lord,
my Strength and my Redeemer.

— A Jewish prayer

52. Day by Day

O most merciful redeemer,
friend and brother,
may we know Thee more clearly,
love Thee more dearly,
and follow Thee more nearly,
day by day.
Amen.

— RICHARD OF CHICHESTER

53. For the Humble Beasts

We pray, Lord,
for the humble beasts
who with us bear the burden and heat of the day,
giving their lives for the well-being of their countries;
and for the wild creatures,
whom you have made wise, strong, and beautiful;
we ask for them your great tenderness of heart,
for you have promised to save both man and beast,
and great is your loving-kindness,
O Savior of the world.

— A Russian Prayer

54. The Acts of John

I want to be saved...and I want to save. Amen.
I want to be set free...and I want to be free. Amen.
I want to be born — and I want to give birth. Amen.
I want to hear...and I want to be heard.
Sweetness dances.
I want to pipe; all of you dance. Amen.
I want to run away...and I want to stay. Amen.
I want to make you beautiful...and I want to be beautiful.
    Amen.
I want to join with you...and I want to be joined. Amen.
I have no house...and I have houses. Amen.
I have no ground...and I have ground. Amen.
I have no temple...and I have temples. Amen.
If you look at me...I will be a lamp. Amen.
If you see me...I will be a mirror. Amen.
If you knock on me...I will be a door. Amen.
If you are a traveler...I will be a road. Amen.
This is my dance...Answer me with dancing.

55. Call Me

Cut through, O Lord, my heart's greed,
and show me your way out.
O Lord, white as jasmine,
after this body has known my Lord
who cares if it feeds a dog
or soaks up water?
Like an elephant lost from his herd
suddenly captured,
remembering his mountains, his Vindhyas,
I remember.
O Lord, white as jasmine, show me your ways.

Call me: Child, come here,
come this way.

— MAHADEVIYAKKA

56. Hymn for the Dead

That day of wrath, that dreadful day,
When heaven and earth shall pass away,
What power shall be the sinner's stay?
How shall he meet that dreadful day?

When, shriveling like a parched scroll,
The flaming heavens together roll;
When louder yet, and yet more dread,
Swells the high trump that wakes the dead!

O! on that day, that wrathful day,
When man to judgment wakes from clay,
Be Thou the trembling sinner's stay,
Though heaven and earth shall pass away!

— SIR WALTER SCOTT

57. Bless My Soul

O my God,
the soul You have placed within me is pure.
You created it, You formed it,
You breathed it within me,
You guard it within me,
You will take it from me in the future
and restore it to me in the future-to-come.
As long as the soul is within me
I thankfully acknowledge You,
O Lord my God and God of my fathers,

Master of all deeds, Lord of all souls.
Blessed are You, O Lord,
who restores souls to the dead.

> — The Talmud

58. An Ancient Jewish Blessing

Blessed are you,
O Lord Our God,
Eternal King,
Who feeds the whole world
With your goodness,
With grace, with loving kindness,
And tender mercy.
You give food to all flesh,
For Your loving kindness endures forever.
Through Your great goodness,
Food has never failed us,
O may it not fail us forever;
For Your name's sake, since you
Nourish and sustain all living things
And do good to all,
And provide food for all your creatures
Whom you have created.
Blessed are You, O Lord,
Who gives food to all.

59. An Arapaho Prayer before Eating

Our father, hear us, and our grandfather.
I mention also all those that shine,
the yellow day, the good wind,
the good timber, and the good earth.

All the animals, listen to me under the ground.
Animals above ground,
and water animals, listen to me.
We shall eat your remnants of food.
Let them be good.
Let there be long breath and life.
Let the people increase,
the children of all ages,
the girls and the boys,
and the men of all ages and the women,
the old men of all ages and the old women.
The food will give us strength
wherever the sun runs.
Listen to us, Father, Grandfather.
We ask thought, heart, love happiness.
We are going to eat.

60. Little Jesus

Little Jesus was Thou shy
Once, and just as small as I?
And what did it feel like to be
Out of heaven and just like me?
Didst Thou sometimes think of there,
And ask where all the angels were?
I should think that I would cry
For my house all made of sky;
I would look about the air,
And wonder where the angels were;
And at waking 'twould distress me —
Not an angel there to dress me.
Hadst Thou ever any toys
Like us little girls and boys?
And didst Thou play in Heaven with all

The angels that were not too tall,
With stars for marbles? Did the things
Play "Can you see me?" through their wings?
And did Thy mother let Thee spoil
Thy robes with playing on our soil?
How nice to have them always new
In Heaven, because 'twas quite clean blue!

— FRANCIS THOMPSON

61. OM

This eternal Word is all;
what was, what is and what shall be,
and what beyond is in eternity.
All is OM.

— The Upanishads

62. Till We See the Chief

Father-Creator, Provider-from-of-old, Ancient-of-days,
fresh-born from the womb of night are we.
In the first dawning of the new day
draw we nigh unto thee.
Forlorn are the eyes till they have seen the Chief.

— Bushman's prayer, South Africa

63. Full of God

If I spent enough time with the tiniest creature —
even a caterpillar —
I would never have to prepare a sermon.
So full of God is every creature.

— MEISTER ECKHART

64. Here I Am

Here I am at Your service,
O Lord, here I am.
Here I am. No partner do You have.
Here I am.
Truly, the praise and the favor is Yours,
and the dominion.
No partner do You have.

— Muslim Prayer, "Talbiyyah"

65. Remember the Fruits

O Lord,
remember not only the men and women of good will,
but also those of ill will.
But do not remember all the suffering they inflicted on us;
remember the fruits we have bought,
thanks to this suffering —
our comradeship, our loyalty, our courage, our generosity,
the greatness of heart which has grown out of all this,
and when they come to judgment
let all the fruits which we have borne be their forgiveness.

— Prayer written by an unknown prisoner in Ravensbruck
concentration camp and left by the body of a dead child

66. For Mother-Love and Father-Care

For mother-love, for father-care;
For brothers strong and sisters fair;
For love at home and school each day;
For guidance lest we go astray —
Father in Heaven, we thank Thee!

— RALPH WALDO EMERSON

67. All Is Silent

All is silent
In the still and soundless air,
I fervently bow
To my almighty God.

— HSIEH PING-HSIN, China

68. So Ancient and So New

Late have I loved you,
O beauty so ancient and so new;
late have I loved you.
You called and cried to me
and broke upon my deafness;
and you sent forth your light
and shone upon me,
and chased away my blindness;
You breathed fragrance upon me,
and I drew in my breath
and do not pant for you:
I tasted you
and I now hunger and thirst for you;
you touched me,
and I have burned for your peace.

— ST. AUGUSTINE

69. Directions

Our Father the Sky,
hear us and make us bold.
O our Mother the Earth,
hear us and give us support.

O Spirit of the East,
send us your Wisdom.
O Spirit of the South,
may we walk your path of life.
O Spirit of the West,
may we always be ready for the long journey.
O Spirit of the North,
purify us with your cleansing winds.

— Sioux Prayer

70. Earth, Teach Me

Earth, teach me stillness
as the grasses are stilled with light.
Earth, teach me suffering
as old stones suffer with memory.
Earth, teach me humility
as blossoms are humble with beginning.
Earth, teach me caring
as the mother who secures her young.
Earth, teach me courage
as the tree which stands all alone.
Earth, teach me limitation
as the ant which crawls on the ground.
Earth, teach me freedom
as the eagle which soars in the sky.
Earth, teach me resignation
as the leaves which die in the fall.
Earth, teach me regeneration
as the seed which rises in the spring.
Earth, teach me to forget myself
as melted snow forgets its life.

Earth, teach me to remember kindness
as the dry fields weep with rain.

— Ute prayer

71. Prayer of an Old Man

Bless, O God,
bless my weather-beaten soul.

— West Indies

72. The Lord's Prayer

This is how you are to pray:
"Our Father in heaven,
Hallowed be your name,
Your kingdom come,
Your will be done
On earth as it is in heaven.
Give us today our daily bread
And forgive us the wrong we have done
As we forgive those who wrong us.
Subject us not to the trial
But deliver us from the evil one."

— From the New American Bible

73. Give and Take

Give us, Lord,
a humble, quiet, peaceable,
patient, tender, and charitable mind,
and in all our thoughts, words, and deeds
a taste of the Holy Spirit.
Give us, Lord,

a lively faith, a firm hope,
a fervent charity, a love of you.
Take from us all lukewarmness in meditation,
dullness in prayer.
Give us fervor and delight
in thinking of you and your grace,
your tender compassion toward me.
The things that we pray for, good Lord,
give us grace to labor for:
through Jesus Christ our Lord.

— ST. THOMAS MORE

74. The Quest

Let me seek you in my desire.
Let me desire you in my seeking.
Let me find you by loving you.
Let me love you when I find you.

— ST. ANSELM

75. Restoration

You made me to find you;
give me strength to see you.
My strength and my weaknesses are in your hands;
preserve my strength and help my weakness.
Where you have opened the door, let me enter in;
where it is shut, open to my knocking.
Let me ever increase in remembering you,
understanding you, loving you,
until you restore me to your perfect pattern.

— ST. AUGUSTINE

76. Answer Me, O God

O Merciful God, who answerest the poor,
Answer us.
O Merciful God, who answerest the lowly in spirit,
Answer us.
O Merciful God, who answerest the broken of heart,
Answer us.
O Merciful God,
Answer us.
O Merciful God,
Have compassion.
O Merciful God,
Redeem.
O Merciful God,
Save.
O Merciful God,
have pity upon us,
Now,
Speedily,
And at a near time.

— Jewish prayer for the Day of Atonement

77. Precious Lord, Take My Hand

Precious Lord, take my hand.
Lead me on. Let me stand.
I am tired. I am weak. I am worn.
Through the storm, through the night,
Lead me on to the light.
Take my hand, precious Lord,
and lead me home.

— African-American Spiritual

78. Small-Craft Prayer

Protect me, O Lord;
My boat is so small,
And your sea is so big.

— A Breton fisherman's prayer

79. A Prayer of Socrates

Dear Pan, and all you other gods who live here,
grant that I may become beautiful within,
and that whatever outward things I have
may be in harmony with the spirit inside me.
May I understand that it is only the wise who are rich,
and may I have only as much money
as a temperate person needs.

Is there anything else that we can ask for, Phaedrus?
For me, that prayer is enough.

80. An Unrestrained Creation Prayer

Bless the Lord, my soul!
Lord God, how great you are,
Clothed in majesty and glory,
Wrapped in light as in a robe!

You stretch out the heavens like a tent,
Above the rains you build your dwelling.
You make the clouds your chariot,
You walk on the wings of the wind,
You make the winds your messengers
And flashing fire your servants.

You founded the earth on its base,
To stand firm from age to age.
You wrapped it with the ocean like a cloak:
The waters stood higher than the mountains.

At your threat they took to flight;
At the voice of your thunder they fled.
They rose over the mountains and they flowed down
To the place which you had appointed.
You set limits they might not pass
Lest they return to cover the earth.

You make springs gush forth in the valleys:
They flow in between the hills.
They give drink to all the beasts of the field;
The wild-asses quench their thirst.
On their banks dwell the birds of heaven;
From the branches they sing their song.

From your dwelling you water the hills;
Earth drinks its fill of your gift.
You make the grass grow for the cattle
And the plants to serve man's needs,

That he may bring forth bread from the earth
And wine to cheer man's heart;
Oil, to make his face shine
And bread to strengthen man's heart.

The trees of the Lord drink their fill,
The cedars he planted on Lebanon;
There the birds build their nests:
On the tree-top the stork has her home.
The goats find a home on the mountains
And rabbits hide in the rocks.

You made the moon to mark the months;
The sun knows the time for its setting.
When you spread the darkness it is night
And all the beasts of the forest creep forth.
The young lions roar for their prey
And ask their food from God.

At the rising of the sun they steal away
And go to rest in their dens.
Man goes forth to his work,
To labor till evening falls.

How many are your works, O Lord!
In wisdom you have made them all.
The earth is full of your riches.

There is the sea, vast and wide,
With its moving swarms past counting,
Living things great and small.
The ships are moving there
And the monsters you made to play with.

All of these look to you
To give them their food in due season.
You give it, they gather it up:
You open your hand, they have their fill.

You hide your face, they are dismayed;
You take back your spirit, they die,
Returning to the dust from which they came.
You send forth your spirit, they are created;
And you renew the face of the earth.

May the glory of the Lord last forever!
May the Lord rejoice in his works!

He looks on the earth and it trembles;
The mountains send forth smoke at his touch.

I will sing to the Lord all my life,
And make music to my God while I live.
May my thoughts be pleasing to him.
I find my joy in the Lord.
Let sinners vanish from the earth
And the wicked exist no more.

Bless the Lord, my soul.

— Psalm 103

81. Good Lord, Deliver Me

From the cowardice that dare not face new truth,
from the laziness that is contented with half truth,
from the arrogance that thinks it knows all truth,
Good Lord, deliver me.

— A Kenyan Prayer

82. I Believe

Lord, I believe;
help thou mine unbelief.

— Mark 9:24

83. I Want to Believe

My Lord, I do not believe;
help thou mine unbelief.

— Samuel Butler

84. Cook Me!

O God,
If I am raw, cook me!
If I am cooked, burn me!

— Kwaja Abdullah Ansari

85. Do Not Forget Me

O Lord,
thou knowest how busy
I must be this day:
if I forget thee,
do not thou forget me.

— Sir Jacob Astley

86. Prayer to St. Michael

St. Michael, Archangel, defend us in battle.
Be our protection against the malice and snares of the
    devil.
Rebuke him, O God, we humbly pray,
and do thou, O Prince of the heavenly hosts,
by the power of God,
thrust into hell Satan and the other evil spirits
who prowl about the world
seeking the ruin of souls. Amen.

— Pope Leo xiii

87. A Prayer in Old Age

God, guard me from those thoughts men think
In the mind alone;

He that sings a lasting song
Thinks in a marrow-bone;
From all that makes a wise old man
That can be praised of all;
O what am I that I should not seem
For the song's sake a fool?
I pray — for fashion's word is out
And prayer comes round again —
That I may seem, though I die old,
A foolish passionate man.

— WILLIAM BUTLER YEATS

88. I Repent

I know that thou canst do every thing,
and that no thought can be withholden from thee.
Who is he that hideth counsel without knowledge?
Therefore have I uttered that I understood not;
things too wonderful for me, which I knew not.
Hear, I beseech thee, and I will speak:
I will demand of thee, and declare thou unto me.
I have heard of thee by the hearing of the ear:
but now mine eyes seeth thee.
Wherefore I abhor myself,
and repent in dust and ashes.

— Job 42:2–6

89. Look at Our Brokenness

Grandfather, look at our brokenness.
We know that in all creation
Only the human family
Has strayed from the Sacred Way.

We know that we are the ones
Who are divided
And we are the ones
Who must come back together
To walk in the Sacred Way.
Grandfather,
Sacred One,
Teach us love, compassion, and honor
That we may heal the earth
And heal each other.

— An Ojibwa Prayer

90. How Long, O Lord?

How long, O Lord? Will you forget me forever?
How long will you hide your face from me?
How long must I bear pain in my soul,
and have sorrow in my heart all day long? . . .
But I trusted in your steadfast love;
my heart shall rejoice in your salvation.
I will sing to the Lord,
because he has dealt bountifully with me.

— Psalm 13:1–2, 5–6

91. A Hymn to God the Father

Wilt Thou forgive that sin where I begun,
Which is my sin, though it were done before?
Wilt Thou forgive that sin, through which I run,
And do run still: though still I do deplore?
When Thou hast done, Thou has not done,
For, I have more.

— JOHN DONNE

92. Jesus' Prayer for His Enemies

My Father,
forgive them,
for they do not realize
what they are doing.

— Luke 23:34

93. At Last

I am not eager, bold
Or strong — all that is past.
I am ready not to do,
At last, at last!

— St. Peter Canisius

94. Eat Me Like Candy

Your prayer should be,
"Break the legs of what I want to happen.
Humiliate my desire.
Eat me like candy.
It's spring, and finally I have no will."

— Jelaluddin Rumi

95. Prayer to Die Easy

I want to die easy when I die.
I want to die easy when I die.
Shout salvation as I fly,
I want to die easy when I die.

— African-American Spiritual

96. Prayer of a Soldier in France

My shoulders ache beneath the pack
(Lie easier, Cross, upon His back.)
I march with feet that burn and smart
(Tread, Holy Feet, upon my heart.)
Men shout at me who may not speak
(They scourged Thy back and smote Thy cheek.)
I may not lift a hand to clear
My eyes of salty drops that sear.
(Then shall my fickle soul forget
Thy Agony of Bloody Sweat?)
My rifle hand is stiff and numb
(From Thy pierced palm red rivers come.)
Lord, Thou didst suffer more for me
Than all the hosts of land and sea.
So let me render back again
This millionth of Thy gift. Amen.

—Joyce Kilmer, author of "Trees,"
died on a World War I battlefield

97. Lead, Kindly Light

Lead, kindly Light, amid the encircling gloom,
Lead thou me on;
The night is dark, and I am far from home,
Lead thou me on.
Keep thou my feet; I do not ask to see
The distant scene; one step enough for me.
I was not ever thus, nor prayed that thou
Shouldst lead me on;
I loved to choose and see my path; but now
Lead thou me on.
I loved the garish day, and, spite of fears,

Pride ruled my will: remember not past years.
So long thy power hath blest me, sure it still
Will lead me on
O'er moon and fen, o'er crag and torrent, till
The night is gone,
And with the morn those Angel faces smile,
Which I have loved long since, and lost awhile.

— JOHN HENRY NEWMAN

98. The Jesus Prayer

Lord Jesus Christ,
Son of God,
have mercy upon me.

— From sixth–seventh centuries

99. Do Right

Will you sweep away the righteous with the wicked?
What if there are fifty righteous people in the city?
Will you really sweep it away and not spare the place
for the sake of the fifty righteous people in it?
Far be it from you to do such a thing —
to kill the righteous with the wicked,
treating the righteous and the wicked alike.
Far be it from you!
Will not the Judge of all the earth do right? . . .
May the Lord not be angry,
but let me speak just once more.
What if only ten can be found there?

— Genesis 18:23–25, 32

100. Do As You Have Promised

O Lord God, why have you showered your blessings
on such an insignificant person as I am?
And now, in addition to everything else,
you speak of giving me an eternal dynasty!
Such generosity is far beyond any human standard!
O Lord God!...

How great you are, Lord God!
We have never heard of any other god like you.
And there is no other god.
What other nation in all the earth
has received such blessings as Israel, your people?
For you have rescued your chosen nation
in order to bring glory to your name.
You have done great miracles to destroy Egypt and its gods.
You chose Israel to be your people forever,
and you became our God.

And now, Lord God,
do as you have promised concerning me and my family.
And may you be eternally honored
when you have established Israel as your people
and have established my dynasty before you.

— 2 Samuel 7:18–19, 22–26

101. Answer Me, O Lord

O Lord, God of Abraham, Isaac and Israel,
let it be known today that you are God in Israel
and that I am your servant
and have done all these things at your command.
Answer me, O Lord, answer me
so that these people will know

that you, O Lord, are God,
and that you are turning their hearts back again.

> — 1 Kings 18:36–37

102. A Little Child's Prayer

Here, a little child I stand,
Heaving up my either hand;
Cold as paddocks though they be,
Here I lift them up to thee,
For a benison to fall
On our meat and on our all.

> — ROBERT HERRICK

103. Have Pity

O Holy Virgin,
in the midst of your glorious days,
do not forget the miseries of the world.
Turn a look of kindness on those who are in suffering
and who cease not to struggle
against the misfortunes of this life.
Have pity on those who love and are separated.
Have pity on the loneliness of the heart.
Have pity on the objects of our tenderness.
Have pity on those who weep, on those who fear.
Give us the hope of peace. Amen.

> — ST. AUGUSTINE

104. Thou Dost Abide

Thou art woman. Thou art man.
Thou art the youth and the maiden too.

Thou as an old man totterest with a staff,
Being born, thou becomest facing in every direction.
Thou art the dark blue bird
and the green parrot with red eyes.
Thou hast the lightning for thy child.
Thou art seasons and seas.
Having no beginning, thou dost abide with immanence,
Wherefrom all beings are born.

— Shvetashvatara Upanishad 4, 3–4

105. If Thou Sendest Me to Hell

Lord, have mercy on me, with all my lawlessness.
Let me pass by Thy judgment.
Do not judge me, for I have condemned myself,
do not condemn me, for I love Thee, O Lord.
I am a wretch, but I love thee.
If Thou sendest me to hell, even there shall I love Thee,
and from there shall I cry out
that I love Thee forever and ever.

— FYODOR DOSTOYEVSKY

106. Let Me Never Be Naughty

O God, who has made everything,
and is so kind and merciful to everything He has made
that tries to be good and to deserve it;
God bless my dear Papa and Mama,
Brothers and Sisters
and all my Relations and Friends.
Make me a good little child,
and let me never be naughty and tell a lie,
which is a mean and shameful thing.

Make me kind to all beggars and poor people,
and never let me be cruel to any dumb creatures,
for if I am cruel to anything, even to a poor little fly,
God, who is so good, will never love me.
And pray God to bless and preserve us all,
this night, and forevermore,
through Jesus Christ our Lord. Amen.

— CHARLES DICKENS, written for his young children

107. High Petitions

And pardon me, good Lord,
that I am so bold as to ask so high petitions,
being so vile a sinful wretch,
and so unworthy to attain the lowest.
But yet, good Lord, such they be,
as I am bounden to wish
and should be nearer the effectual desire of them,
if my manifold sins were not the let.

— SIR THOMAS MORE, written while a prisoner
in the Tower of London

108. Correct Me, Lord

O Lord, I know that it is not within the power of a man
to map his life and plan his course —
so you correct me, Lord; but please be gentle.
Don't do it in your anger, for I will die.
Pour out your fury on the nations who don't obey the Lord,
for they have destroyed Israel
and made a wasteland of this entire country.

— Jeremiah 10:23–25

109. You Hear Me

Father, I thank you that you have heard me.
I knew that you always hear me,
but I said this for the benefit of the people standing here,
that they may believe that you sent me.

—John 11:41–42

110. Our Only Help

We take refuge in thee,
thou art our only help.
O Lord, we beseech thee to take birth as a man
in order to destroy the enemy of man and gods.

— Ramayana 1, 15

111. To Find Something Lost

St. Anthony, St. Anthony, come around.
Something's lost and must be found.

112. After Finding

St. Anthony, St. Anthony, you we praise.
We thank you for your wondrous ways.

113. A God of Forgiveness

You are a God ready to forgive, gracious and merciful,
slow to anger and abounding in steadfast love.

—Nehemiah 9:17

114. I Will Sing

I will sing of well-founded Earth,
mother of all, eldest of all beings.
She feeds all creatures that are in the world,
all that go upon the goodly land,
and all that are in the paths of the seas,
and all that fly:
all these are fed from her store.
Through you, O Queen,
men are blessed in their children and in their harvests.

— HOMER

115. The Lord of the Worlds

In the Name of God,
the Merciful, the Compassionate.
Praise belongs to God,
the Lord of the worlds,
the Merciful, the Compassionate,
Master of the Day of Judgment.

— Koran 1, 1–3

116. Jesus' Prayer of Feeling Totally Abandoned

My God, my God, why have you forsaken me?

— Mark 15:34

117. In You All My Sad Soul-Hurts Vanish

I have eaten at the head of the table,
and now I wish to die at the head of my brothers,
and mix my blood with theirs.

With them I wish to come to know the life
that holds neither suffering nor pain,
that knows not the tyranny of victims.
In that life I shan't be flayed
by the threats of kings or the terrors of prefectures.
Nor will anyone be able to drag me before the tribunal
or make me tremble out of fear.
In you shall I correct the errors of my past,
O life of truth, in you my weary limbs will find repose,
O Christ, sacred oil of our unction.
In you all my sad soul-hurts vanish,
for you are truly the cup of my salvation.
You shall dry these tears from my eyes,
O consolation and joy!

... The cross of our Lord protect those who belong to Jesus
and strengthen your hearts in faith to Christ
in hardship and ease, in life and in death, now and forever.

— SIMEON BAR SABBAE,
bishop in Persia, martyred fourth century

118. Yes, Lord

Yes, Lord, you are the God of all.
Yes, Lord, you are the King of all.
Yes, Lord, you are the Almighty.
Yes, Lord you are the Governor of all.
Yes, Lord, you are the Savior of all.
Yes, Lord, you are the Judge of all.
Yes, Lord, you are the Life-giver of all.
Yes, Lord, you are the keeper of all.
Yes, Lord, you are the nourisher of all.

— Patriarch of Antioch, fifth century

119. Our Strength Is in You, God

O God, forasmuch as our strength is in you,
mercifully grant that your Holy Spirit
may in all things direct and rule our hearts,
through Jesus Christ our Lord.

— From the Gelasian Sacramentary, eighth century

120. You Guide Us Better

Lord God Almighty,
shaper and ruler of all creatures,
we pray for your great mercy,
that you guide us better than we have done, toward you.
And guide us to your will, to the need of our soul,
better than we can ourselves.
And steadfast our mind toward your will
and to our soul's need.
And strengthen us against the temptations of the devil,
and far from us all lust, and every unrighteousness,
and shield us against our foes, seen and unseen.
And teach us to do your will,
that we may inwardly love you before all things,
with a pure mind.
For you are our maker, our redeemer,
our help, our comfort, our trust, our hope;
praise and glory be to you now,
ever and ever, world without end.

— ALFRED THE GREAT

121. The Knower and the Known

Thou are the Primal God, the Ancient Spirit,
Thou are the Supreme Treasure-house of this universe,

Thou are the knower, and the known, the highest Home,
By thee the universe is pervaded, O thou of infinite form.

— Bhagavad Gita, 11, 38

122. Moses' Hymn of Victory

I will offer praise to the Lord,
for he has been triumphant and shown forth his glory;
horse and chariot he has hurled into the sea.
The Lord is the source of my strength and my courage;
he has been my Savior.
The Lord is my God, and I offer him praise;
He is the God of my father,
and I sing of his marvelous deeds.
The Lord has proved himself a warrior; Lord is his name.
The chariots and the army of Pharaoh he cast into the sea.

At a breath of your anger the waters cascaded;
the waters ceased to flow and converged together,
forming a barrier in the midst of the sea.
The enemy had boasted:
"We will relentlessly pursue them,
and when we overtake them,
we will divide the spoils and be satiated with them;
we will draw our swords and gather up our plunder."
But when you caused the wind to blow,
the sea swept over them;
they sank like lead in the swirling waters.

Who can compare to you among the gods, O Lord?
Who can begin to comprehend how magnificent is your
    holiness?
O worker of wonders, whose renown is incomparable,
when you stretched out your right hand,

the earth consumed our enemies.
You showed mercy by leading the people you had redeemed;
you proved your strength by guiding them to your holy
   dwelling.
Then you brought them in and gave them the mountain of
   your inheritance as their dwelling —
the place that you chose for your throne, O Lord,
the sanctuary established by your hands.
The Lord shall rule forever and ever.

—Exodus 15:1–4a, 8–13, 17–18

123. Brotherly Kindness

Pour upon us, O Lord,
the spirit of brotherly kindness and peace;
so that, sprinkled with the dew of your benediction,
we may be made glad by your glory and grace;
through Christ our Lord.

—From the Sarum Breviary, eleventh century

124. God with Me

God be in my head
And in my understanding.

—Sarum Missal, 1514

125. Thy Mighty Hand

Essence beyond essence, Nature increate,
Framer of the world, I set thee, Lord, before my face.
I lift up my soul to thee, I worship thee on my knees,
And humble myself under thy mighty hand.

—Lancelot Andrews

126. Rid My Mind of the Business

Give me the grace, good Lord,
to set the world at naught;
to set my mind fast upon Thee
and not to hang upon the blast of men's mouths.
To be content to be solitary.
Not to long for worldly company
but utterly to cast off the world
and rid my mind of the business thereof.

— St. Thomas More

127. With You I Am Rich Enough

Take, our Lord, and receive my entire liberty,
my memory, my understanding, and my whole will.
All that I am, all that I have, you have given me
and I will give it back again to you
to be disposed of according to your good pleasure.
Give me only your love and your grace;
with you I am rich enough,
nor do I ask for aught besides. Amen.

— St. Ignatius Loyola

128. True Prosperity

We pray for the people,
that they make not themselves over-wise;
but be persuaded by reason,
and yield to the authority of their superiors.

We pray for the kingdoms of the world,
their stability and peace;
for our own nation, kingdom, and empire,

that they may abide in prosperity and happiness,
and be delivered from all peril and disaster.

For the King, O Lord, save him;
O Lord, give him prosperity,
compass him with the shield of truth and glory,
speak good things unto him,
in behalf of your church and people.

Unto all men everywhere give your grace and blessing;
through Jesus Christ.

— LANCELOT ANDREWS

129. We Talk of Religion and Pretend Unto It

Infinite and eternal Majesty!
Author and fountain of being and blessedness!
How little do we poor sinful creatures know of you
or the way to serve and please you!
We talk of religion and pretend unto it;
but alas! how few are there that know
and consider what it means!
How easily do we mistake the affections of our nature
and the issues of self-love
for those divine graces which alone
can render us acceptable in your sight!

It may justly grieve me to consider
that I should have wandered so long
and contented myself so often
with vain shadows and false images of piety and religion;
yet I cannot but acknowledge and adore your goodness,
who has been pleased in some measures to open my eyes
and let me see what mighty improvements
my nature is capable of...

Let me never cease my endeavors
till that new and divine nature prevail
in my soul and Christ be formed within me.

— Henry Scougal

130. One Thing We Ask of You

We must praise your goodness,
that you have left nothing undone to draw us to yourself.
But one thing we ask of you, our God,
not to cease your work in our improvement.
Let us tend toward you, no matter by what means,
and be fruitful in good works,
for the sake of Jesus Christ our Lord.

— Ludwig Von Beethoven

131. You're Everywhere!

Whither shall I go from thy spirit?
Or whither shall I flee from thy presence?
If I ascend up into heaven, thou art there.
If I make my bed in hell, behold, thou art there.

— Psalm 139:7–8

132. Prayer of "Giving Credit Where It Is Due"

We have been blessed with a strong city;
the Lord has established walls and ramparts to protect us.
Throw open the gates
to allow entrance to a nation of firm purpose;
peace is its reward for its trust in you.
Have trust in the Lord forever,
for he will be our Rock forever.

The just travel along a smooth road;
the path of the just you have made level.
For the path you wish us to follow
and your judgments, O Lord,
we look to you.
Your name and your title are our soul's desire.
My soul yearns for your presence during the night;
yes, my innermost spirit keeps vigil for you.
When the earth encounters the dawn of your judgment,
those who dwell there will comprehend
the meaning of justice.
O Lord, you are the source of our peace,
for you have accomplished everything we have done.

—Isaiah 26:1–4, 7–9, 12

133. With Malice toward None

Grant, O merciful God,
that with malice toward none, with charity to all,
with firmness in the right as you give us to see the right,
we may strive to finish the work we are in;
to bind up the nation's wounds;
to care for him who shall have borne the battle
and for his widow and his orphan;
to do all which may achieve and cherish
a just and lasting peace
among ourselves and with all nations.

— Abraham Lincoln

134. Like a Rock

Incline your ear to me; rescue me speedily.
Be a rock of refuge for me,

a strong fortress to save me.
You are indeed my rock and my fortress;
for your name's sake lead me and guide me . . .
for you are my refuge.

— Psalm 31:2–4

135. Things That Go Bump in the Night

From ghoulies and ghosties
and long-leggety beasties
And things that go bump in the night,
Good Lord, deliver us!

— Scottish prayer

136. Excellence in Business and Government

As long as man is set against man
in a struggle for wealth,
help the men in business to make their contest,
as far as may be, a test of excellence,
by which even the defeated
may be spurred to better work. . . .
Establish in unshaken fidelity
all who hold in trust the savings of others. . . .
Cause them to realize
that they serve not themselves alone,
but hold high public functions,
and do save them from betraying the interests of the many
of their own enrichment,
lest a new tyranny grow up in a land
that is dedicated to freedom . . .

— WALTER RAUSCHENBUSCH

137. Seek and Find

O Lord, you are so good to the soul who seeks you,
what must you be to the one who finds you?

— BERNARD OF CLAIRVAUX

138. Not Because of Heaven

My God, I love Thee;
Not because I hope for heaven thereby.

— EDWARD CASWALL

139. Prayer for Soldiers and Sailors

Bless, O Lord, our soldiers and sailors,
of whatever rank or quality.
Grant that in the midst of every temptation which besets
    them
they may fight manfully against the world, the flesh, and
    the devil;
and, resisting all evil by the spirit of your ... strength,
may acquire true courage in the victory of faith.
Prosper them in the maintenance of our country's honor,
and keep them safe from enemies spiritual and temporal,
that they may glorify you upon the earth,
until they are called to rest in the triumph of your glory;
through Jesus Christ our Lord.

— RICHARD MEUX BENSON

140. I Am Ready for All

Father, I abandon myself into your hands;
do with me what you will.

Whatever you may do, I thank you.
I am ready for all, I accept all.
Let only your will be done in me,
and in all your creatures —
I wish no more than this, O Lord.

Into your hands
I commend my soul;
I offer it to you
with all the love of my heart,
for I love you, Lord,
and so I need to give myself,
to surrender myself,
into your hands
without reserve
and with boundless confidence,
for you are my Father.

— Brother Charles of Jesus

141. Mercy

Have mercy on me, O God,
according to your steadfast love;
according to your abundant mercy
blot out my transgressions.
Wash me thoroughly from my iniquity
and cleanse me from my sin.

— Psalm 51:1–2

142. Peace in Our Time

Grant peace, we pray, in mercy, Lord;
Peace in our time, oh send us!

For there is none on earth but you,
None other to defend us.
You only, Lord,
can fight for us. Amen.

— MARTIN LUTHER

143. I Find No Rest

My God, my God,
why have you forsaken me?
Why are you so far from helping me,
from the words of my groaning?
O my God, I cry by day,
but you do not answer,
and by night,
but find no rest.

— Psalm 22:1–2

144. Prayer in Time of Great Distress

Do not forget, O Lord,
what misfortune has overtaken us;
look upon us and realize our disgrace.
The lands of our inheritance
have been turned over to strangers,
our homes to foreigners.
We have become orphans, without fathers;
our mothers are now widowed.
We are forced to purchase the water we drink,
we must buy our own wood.

The yokes of those who drive us strangle our necks;
we are exhausted but allowed no time to rest....

Our ancestors, who sinned, have now all died,
but we continue to bear their guilt.
There is no longer joy in our hearts;
where we once danced we now mourn.
Our heads are no longer adorned with garlands;
wretchedness has befallen us, for we have sinned.
Our hearts are sick about this situation;
the mere thought of it causes our eyes to grow dim.

You, O Lord, will reign forever;
your throne stands invincible from age to age.
Why, then, have you forgotten us
and abandoned us for so long a time?
Lead us back to you, O Lord,
so that we may be restored to your friendship;
give us once again such days as we formerly experienced.

—Lamentations 5:1–7, 15–17, 19–21

145. Rise Up, My Love

Rise up, my love, my fair one, and come away.
For, lo, the winter is past, the rain is over and gone,
The flowers appear on the earth,
the time of the singing of birds is come,
and the voice of the turtle is heard in our land.
The fig tree putteth forth her green figs,
and the vines with the tender grape give a good smell.
Arise, my love, my fair one, and come away.
O my dove, that art in the clefts of the rock,
in the secret places of the stairs,
let me see thy countenance, let me hear thy voice;
for sweet is thy voice, and thy countenance is comely.

—Song of Solomon 2:10–14

146. You Merely Look at Me

And now my soul is poured out within me;
days of affliction have taken hold of me.
The night racks my bones,
and the pain that gnaws me takes no rest...
I cry to you and you do not answer me;
I stand and you merely look at me.

— Job 30:16–17, 20

147. A Relative I Am!

Hear me, four quarters of the world — a relative I am!
Give me the strength to walk the soft earth,
a relative to all that is!
Give me the eyes to see and the strength to understand
that I may be like you....
Great Spirit, Great Spirit, my Grandfather,
all over the earth the faces of living things are all alike.
With tenderness have these come up out of the ground.
Look upon these faces of children without number
and with children in their arms
that they may face the winds and walk the good road
to the day of quiet.

— Black Elk

148. Crow Song (Native American)

You Above,
if there be one there who knows what is going on,
repay me today for the distress I have suffered.
Inside the Earth,
if there be one there who knows what is going on,
repay me for the distress I have suffered.

The One Who Causes Things,
whoever he be,
I have now had my fill of life.
Grant me death, my sorrows are overabundant.
I do not want to live long;
were I to live long, my sorrows would be overabundant.
I do not want it!

149. Navajo Birth Chant

May I give birth to Pollen Boy,
May I give birth to Cornbeetle Boy,
May I give birth to Long-Life Boy,
May I give birth to Happiness Boy!

150. Prayer to Our Keeper

Lord of the Mountain,
Reared within the Mountain
Young Man, Chieftain,
Here's a young man's prayer!
Hear a prayer for cleanness.
Keeper of the strong rain,
Drumming on the mountain;
Lord of the small rain
That restores the earth in newness;
Keeper of the clean rain,
Hear a prayer of wholeness.

Young Man, Chieftain,
Hear a prayer for fleetness.
Keeper of the deer's way,
Reared among the eagles,
Clear my feet of slothness.

Keeper of the paths of men,
Hear a prayer for straightness.

Hear a prayer for courage.
Lord of the thin peaks,
Reared amid the thunder;
Keeper of the headlands
Holding up the harvest,
Keeper of the strong rocks
Hear a prayer for staunchness.

Young Man, Chieftain,
Spirit of the Mountain!

— Navajo prayer

151. A Family Prayer

Lord, behold our family here assembled.
We thank you for this place in which we dwell,
for the love that unites us,
for the peace accorded us this day,
for the hope with which we expect the morrow;
for the health, the work, the food,
and the bright skies that make our lives delightful;
for our friends in all parts of the earth.
Amen.

— ROBERT LOUIS STEVENSON

152. Enable Me

Lord, I cannot do this unless You enable me.

— BROTHER LAWRENCE

153. Prayer for a Stiff-Necked People

If now I have found favor in your sight,
O Lord, I pray, let the Lord walk with us.
Although this is a stiff-necked people,
pardon our iniquity and our sin,
and take us for your inheritance.

—MOSES (Exodus 34:8–9)

154. Greenland Eskimo Chant for Birth

That she was taken out of her mother, thanks be for that!
That she, the little one, was taken out of her,
we say, thanks be for that!

155. Shine Through Me

Dear Jesus, help me to spread your fragrance everywhere.
Flood my soul with your spirit and your life.
Penetrate and possess my whole being so utterly
that all my life may be only a radiance of you.
Shine through me and be so in me
that every soul I come in contact with
may feel your presence in my soul.
Let them look up and see no longer me but only Jesus.

—CARDINAL JOHN HENRY NEWMAN

156. Prayer for a Good Home Life

Blessed are you who fear the Lord,
who follow his path.
For you shall enjoy the fruits of your labor;
you shall be blessed with happiness and prosperity.
Your wife shall be like a fertile vine

that blossoms in your home;
your children shall be like olive plants
as they gather around your table.
In the same way will the person be blessed
who fears the Lord.

—Psalm 128

157. A Thanksgiving Proclamation

Inasmuch as the great Father has given us this year
an abundant harvest of Indian corn, wheat,
beans, squashes, and garden vegetables
and has made the forest to abound with game,
and the sea with fish and clams, ...
I, your magistrate, do proclaim
that all ye Pilgrims, with your wives and your little ones,
do gather at ye meeting house, on ye hill ...
and render to ye Almighty God for all His blessings.

— WILLIAM BRADFORD, Plymouth, Massachusetts,
November 29, 1623

158. Bless Our Labors

Great Spirit, who hast blessed the earth
that it should be fruitful
and bring forth whatsoever is needed for the life of us,
and has commanded us to work with quietness,
and eat our own bread;
Bless the labors of those who till the fields
and grant such seasonable weather
that we may gather in the fruits of the earth.

— Adapted from *The Book of Common Prayer*

159. An Old Irish Prayer

May our neighbors respect us,
may trouble neglect us,
may the angels protect us,
and may heaven accept us!

160. Full of Bliss

Now may every living thing,
young or old, weak or strong,
living near or far, known or unknown,
living or departed or yet unborn,
may every living thing be full of bliss.

— BUDDHA

161. A Mennonite Blessing

Thank you for the wind and rain,
and sun and pleasant weather,
thank you for this our food
and that we are together.

162. A Sanskrit Blessing

The food is Brahma (creative energy);
its essence is Vishnu (preservative energy);
the eater is Shiva (destructive energy);
No sickness due to food can come
to one who eats with this knowledge.

163. In This Season of Thy Thanksgiving

Give us thankful hearts...
in this the season of Thy Thanksgiving.

May we be thankful for health and strength,
for sun and rain and peace.

Let us seize the day and the opportunity
and strive for that greatness of spirit that measures life
not by its disappointments but by its possibilities.

— W. E. B. Du Bois

164. Jesus' Prayer for All Believers

Father, I do not pray simply for those
whom you entrusted to me;
I also pray for those who will believe in me
through their testimony,
so that all may be one,
as you, Father, are in me and I am in you.
May they be one in us
in order that the world may come to believe
that you sent me.
I have given them the glory you gave me
so that they may be one as we are one —
I living in them, you living in me —
and thus their unity may be complete.
In this way the world will know that you sent me
and that you loved them just as you loved me.

Father, all those you entrusted to my care
I wish to be in my company in heaven
and to behold my glory,
which you bestowed on me
because of the love you had for me before
the creation of the world.

Just Father,
those you entrusted to me do not know you,

but I know you,
and they are aware that you sent me.
To them I have made known your name,
and I will continue to do so,
in order that the love you have for me
may live in them,
and I too may live in them.

—John 17:20–26

165. God's Own

God within me, God without.
How can I ever be in doubt?
I am the sower and the sown.
God's self unfolding and God's own.

—From a Runic writing

166. Revive My Soul

There is a balm in Gilead to make the wounded whole;
there is a balm in Gilead to heal the sin-sick soul.
Sometimes I feel discouraged, and think my work's in vain,
but then the Holy Spirit revives my soul again.
If you can't preach like Peter, if you can't pray like Paul,
Just tell the love of Jesus, and say he died for all.

—African-American Spiritual

167. We Alone!

My God, my God, let me for once look on thee
As though nought else existed, we alone!

And as creation crumbles, my soul's spark
Expands till I can say — even for myself
I need thee and I feel thee and I love thee.

> — ROBERT BROWNING

168. Be Verily Present with Me

Grant, O Lord,
that I may be so ravished in the wonder of thy love
that I may forget myself and all things;
may feel neither prosperity nor adversity;
may not fear to suffer all the pain in the world
rather than be parted from thee.

O let me find thee more inwardly and verily present with
me than I am with myself;
and make me most circumspect how I do use myself in the
presence of thee, my holy Lord.

> — ROBERT LEIGHTON

169. Lord, Make Me See

Lord, make me see thy glory in every place.

> — MICHELANGELO

170. Grant Me Strength in Weakness

Lord, Jesus Christ, king of kings,
you have power over life and death.
You know what is secret and what is hidden,
and neither our thought nor our feelings
are concealed from you.
Cure me of duplicity; I have done evil before you.

Now my life declines from day to day and my sins increase.
O Lord, God of souls and bodies,
you know the extreme frailty of my soul and my flesh.
Grant me strength in my weakness, O Lord,
and sustain me in my misery.

Give me a grateful soul
that I may never cease to recall your benefits,
O Lord most bountiful.
Be not mindful of my many sins,
but forgive me all my misdeeds.

O Lord, disdain not my prayer —
the prayer of a wretched sinner;
sustain me with your grace until the end,
that it may protect me as in the past.
It is your grace which has taught me wisdom;
blessed are they who follow her ways,
for they shall receive the crown of glory.

In spite of my unworthiness,
I praise and glorify you, O Lord,
for your mercy to me is without limit.
You have been my help and my protection.
May the name of your majesty be praised forever.
To you, our God, be glory. Amen.

> — St. Ephraem the Deacon,
> born in present-day Syria (306–73)

171. Pray in Me

Teach me to pray,
pray thou thyself in me.

> — François Fenelon

172. This Dullness in Praying

Take from me, good Lord, this lukewarm fashion,
or rather key-cold manner of meditation
and this dullness in praying unto thee.
And give me warmth, delight, and quickness
in thinking upon thee.

> — SIR THOMAS MORE, written while a prisoner
> in the Tower of London

173. Pray Often

Teach us to pray often, that we may pray oftener.

> — JEREMY TAYLOR

174. Psalm 23

The Lord is my shepherd, I shall not want.
He makes me to lie down in green pastures;
he leads me beside still waters; he restores my soul.
He leads me in right paths for his name's sake.

Even though I walk through the darkest valley,
I fear no evil; for you are with me;
your rod and your staff — they comfort me.

> — Psalm 23:1–4

175. Unabashed Male's Unabashed Prayer of Thanks

Blessed art thou, O Lord our God, King of the universe,
who hast not made me a woman.

> — *Hebrew Authorized Daily Prayer Book*

176. Thanks for Listening

I thank you, Father, that you listen to me.

—John 11:41

177. I'm Worth More Than Ever!

I bless God I do find
that I am worth more than ever yet I was,
which is 6,200 pounds,
for which the Holy Name of God be praised!

—SAMUEL PEPYS, Diary, October 31, 1666

178. You Know All My Thoughts

O Lord, thou hast me searched and known:
Thou know'st my sitting down
And rising up. Yea all my thoughts
Afar to thee are known.

My soul, praise, praise, praise the Lord!
O God, thou art great:
In fathomless works
Thyself thou dost hide.
Before thy dark wisdom
And power uncreate,
Man's mind, that dare praise thee,
In fear must abide.

—ROBERT BRIDGES

179. Thank You, God, for This Middle-Earth

Now we must praise the ruler of heaven,
the might of the Lord and his purpose of mind,

the work of the glorious Father;
for he, God eternal, established each wonder,
he, holy creator, first fashioned the heavens
as a roof for the children of earth.
And then our guardian, the everlasting Lord,
adorned this middle-earth for me.
Praise the almighty king of heaven.

— CAEDMON, seventh century

180. Draw Boundless Love from Me, O Lord

Lord, how much juice you can squeeze from a single grape.
How much water you can draw from a single well.
How great a fire you can kindle from a tiny spark.
How great a tree you can grow from a tiny seed.
My soul is so dry that by itself it cannot pray;
yet you can draw from it boundless love
for you and for my neighbor.
My soul is so cold that by itself it has no joy;
yet you can light the fire of heavenly joy within me.
My soul is so feeble that by itself it has no faith;
yet by your power my faith grows to a great height.
Thank you for prayer, for love, for joy, for faith;
let me always be prayerful, loving, joyful, faithful.

— GUIGO THE CARTHUSIAN, died 1188

181. A Prayer of St. Patrick

Our God, God of all men,
God of heaven and earth, seas and rivers,
God of sun and moon, of all the stars,
God of high mountain and lowly valleys,
God over heaven, and in heaven, and under heaven.

He has a dwelling in heaven and earth and sea
and in all things that are in them.
He inspires all things, he quickens all things.
He is over all things, he supports all things.
He makes the light of the sun to shine,
He surrounds the moon and the stars,
He has made wells in the arid earth,
placed dry islands in the sea.
He has a Son co-eternal with himself. . . .
And the Holy Spirit breathes in them;
not separate are the Father and the Son and Holy Spirit.

182. Thank You for Joy

O God, I thank thee for all the joy I have had in life.

— BYRHTNOTH, tenth century

183. Thy Mercy Never Dies

Though waves and storms go o'er my head,
Though strength and health and friends be gone,
Though joys be withered all, and dead,
Though every comfort be withdrawn,
On this my steadfast soul relies, —
Father! Thy mercy never dies.

— JOHANN A. ROTHE

184. Thou Art More Than They

Strong Son of God, immortal Love,
Whom we, that have not seen thy face,
By faith, and faith alone, embrace,
Believing where we cannot prove;

Thine are these orbs of light and shade;
Thou madest life in man and brute;
Thou madest death; and lo, thy foot
Is on the skull which thou hast made.

Thou wilt not leave us in the dust:
Thou madest man, he knows not why,
He thinks he was not made to die;
And thou hast made him: thou art just.

Thou seemest human and divine,
The highest, holiest manhood, thou:
Our wills are ours, we know not how;
Our wills are ours, to make them thine.

Our little systems have their day;
They have their day and cease to be:
They are broken lights of thee,
And thou, O Lord, art more than they.

— ALFRED, LORD TENNYSON

185. Give Us Peace

Lord, teach us to number our days,
that we may apply our hearts unto wisdom.
Lighten, if it be thy will,
the pressures of this world's cares.
Above all, reconcile us to thy will,
and give us a peace
in which the world cannot take away;
through Jesus Christ our Lord.
Amen.

— THOMAS CHALMERS

186. You Are My Sunshine

Be thou a light unto my eyes, music to mine ears,
sweetness to my taste, and full contentment to my heart.
Be thou my sunshine in the day, my food at table,
my repose in the night, my clothing in nakedness,
and my succor in all necessities.
Lord, Jesus, I give thee my body, my soul,
my substance, my fame, my friends, my liberty and my life.
Dispose of me and all that is mine
as it may seem best to thee
and to the glory of thy blessed name.

— JOHN COSIN

187. Let's Make a Deal

God of Clotilda,
if you grant me victory,
I shall become a Christian.

— CLOVIS, 465–511, legendary vow before battle,
to the Christian God of his wife, Clotilda

188. Prayer to Give and Not to Count the Cost

Teach us, good Lord,
to serve Thee as Thou deservest:
to give and not to count the cost;
to fight and not to heed the wounds;
to toil and not to seek for rest;
to labor and not ask for any reward
save that of knowing that we do Thy will.

— ST. IGNATIUS LOYOLA

189. Prayer for America

Long may our land be bright,
With freedom's holy light;
Protect us by thy might,
Great God, our King!

— From "America," by SAMUEL FRANCIS SMITH

190. Come to My Aid

Show me, O Lord, your mercy and delight my heart with it.
Let me find you, since I seek you with such great longing.

Behold, here is the man whom the robbers seized,
        mishandled, and left half dead on the road to Jericho.
O kind-hearted Samaritan! Come to my aid.

I am the sheep who wandered into the wilderness;
seek after me and bring me back to your fold.
Do with me according to your will
that I may abide with you all the days of my life
and praise you with all those who are now with you in
        heaven, for all eternity. Amen.

— ST. JEROME

191. Forgive Our Foolish Ways!

Dear Lord and Father of mankind,
Forgive our foolish ways!
Reclothe us in our rightful mind,
In purer lives Thy service find,
In deeper reverence, praise.

— JOHN GREENLEAF WHITTIER

192. Take It All

Take, Lord, and receive all my liberty,
my memory, my understanding, and all my will,
all that I have and possess.
Thou hast given them to me;
to thee, O Lord, I restore them;
all things are thine, dispose of them according to thy will.
Give me thy love and thy grace, for this is enough for me.

— St. Ignatius Loyola

193. Use Me a Little

O Jesus, fill me with thy love now,
and I beseech thee,
accept me, and use me a little for thy glory.
O do, do, I beseech thee, accept me and my service,
and take thou all the glory.

— David Livingstone

194. Open the Eyes of Our Mind

O Lord and lover of all men,
shine in our hearts the pure light of your divine knowledge,
and open the eyes of our mind
to the understanding of your gospel teaching.

Instill in us the fear of your blessed commandments,
that, trampling upon all carnal desires,
we may enter on a spiritual life,
willing and doing all that is your good pleasure.

For you are the light of our souls and of our bodies,
Christ O God, and we give glory to you,

together with your eternal Father
and your all-holy, good, and life-giving Spirit,
now and forever, world without end. Amen.

— St. John Chrysostom

195. Prayer for Child-Like Love

Most loving Lord, give me a childlike love of thee,
which shall cast out all fear.

— Edward Bouverie Pusey

196. "The Jesus Prayer"

Lord, Jesus Christ,
Son of the Living God,
have mercy on me, a sinner.

— St. Macarius, Egyptian Desert Father, fourth century

197. Prayer for My Child

O Lord my God, shed the light of your love on my child.
Keep him safe from all illness and all injury.
Enter his tiny soul,
and comfort him with your peace and joy.
He is too young to speak to me,
and to my ears his cries and gurgles
are meaningless nonsense.
But to your ears they are prayers.
His cries are cries for your blessing.
His gurgles are gurgles of delight at your grace.
Let him as a child learn the way of your commandments.
As an adult let him live the full span of life,
serving your kingdom on earth.

And finally in his old age,
let him die in the sure and certain knowledge
of your salvation.
I do not ask that he be wealthy, powerful, or famous.
Rather I ask that he be poor in spirit,
humble in action, and devout in worship.
Dear Lord, smile upon him.

— JOHANN STARCK

198. O God, Our Help in Ages Past

O God, our help in ages past,
Our hope for years to come.
Our shelter from the stormy blast,
And our eternal home.

— Psalm 90, adapted by ISAAC WATTS

199. Prayer Upon the Death of a Young Son

O God, to me whom am left to mourn his departure,
grant that I may not sorrow as one without hope
for my beloved who sleeps in you;
but, as always remembering his courage,
and the love that united us on earth,
I may begin again with new courage
to serve you more fervently
who are the only source of true love and true fortitude;
that when I have passed a few more days
in this valley of tears and this shadow of death,
supported by your rod and staff, I may see him face to face,
in those pastures and beside those waters of comfort
where I believe he already walks with you.

O Shepherd of the sheep,
have pity on this darkened soul of mine.

> — EDWARD WHITE BENSON
> written on the death of his young son, Martin, in 1877

200. Benedict's Prayer to Live Life God's Way

O Lord, I place myself in your hands
and dedicate myself to you.
I pledge myself to do your will in all things —
to love the Lord God with all my heart,
all my soul, all my strength.

Not to kill or steal; not to covet or bear false witness.
To honor all persons.
Not to do to another
what I would not have done to myself.
To chastise the body and not to seek after pleasures.

To love fasting and to relieve the poor;
to clothe the naked and to visit the sick;
to bury the dead and to help those in trouble.
To console the sorrowing
and to hold myself aloof from worldly ways.
To prefer nothing to the love of Christ.

Not to give way to anger nor to foster a desire for revenge;
not to entertain deceit in the heart
nor to make a false peace;
not to forsake charity nor to swear, lest I swear falsely.

To speak the truth with heart and tongue
and not to return evil for evil;
to do no evil and, indeed,
even to bear patiently any injury done to me.

To love my enemies
and not to curse those who curse me —
but rather to bless them.

To bear persecution for justice's sake and not to be proud.
Not to delight in intoxicating drink,
nor to be an over-eater;
not to be lazy or slothful;
not to be a murmurer or a detractor.
To put my trust in God
and to refer the good I see in myself to God;
to refer any evil in myself,
and to fear the day of judgment.
To be in dread of hell
and to desire eternal life with ardent longing;
to keep death before my eyes daily
and to keep constant watch over my words and deeds.

To remember that God sees me everywhere
and so to call upon Christ
for defense against evil thoughts that spring up in my heart.
To guard my tongue against wicked speech
and, indeed, to avoid much speaking.
To avoid idle talk and not try to be considered clever.

To read only what is good to read
and to look at only what is good to see.
To pray often.
To ask forgiveness daily for my sins
and to look for ways to amend my life.
To obey my superiors in all legitimate things,
not to be thought holy so much as to be holy.

To fulfill the commandments of God through good works.
To love chastity and to hate no one.

Not to be jealous or envious of anyone,
nor to love strife and pride.
To honor the aged and to pray for my enemies.
To make peace after a quarrel before sunset
and never to despair of your mercy, O God of mercy. Amen.

— St. Benedict of Nursia

201. Godpeace

Calm Soul of all things! make it mine
To feel, amid the city's jar,
That there abides a peace of thine,
Man did not make, and can not mar.

— Matthew Arnold

202. Hear Their Cries, O Lord

May the cry of widows, orphans
and destitute children
enter into thine ears, O most loving Savior.
Comfort them with a mother's tenderness,
shield them from the perils of this world,
and bring them at last to thy heavenly home.

— John Cosin

203. Despite Everything, I Thank You

O God, you have dealt very mysteriously with us.
We have been passing through deep waters;
our feet were well-nigh gone.
But though you slay us, yet will we trust in you. . . .
They are gone from us. . . .
You have reclaimed the lent jewels.

Yet, O Lord, shall I not thank you now?
I will thank you
not only for the children you have left to us,
but for those you have reclaimed.
I thank you for the blessing of the last ten years,
and for all the sweet memories of these lives....
I thank you for the full assurance
that each has gone to the arms of the Good Shepherd,
whom each loved according to the capacity of her years.
I thank you for the bright hopes of a happy reunion,
when we shall meet to part no more.
O Lord, for Jesus Christ's sake,
comfort our desolate hearts.
May we be a united family in heart
through the communion of saints;
through Jesus Christ our Lord

> — ARCHIBALD CAMPBELL TAIT
> (between March 11 and April 8, 1856, Tait and his wife
> lost five of their six daughters to scarlet fever)

204. Make Me a King

I am only a spark. Make me a fire.
I am only a string. Make me a lyre.
I am only a drop. Make me a fountain.
I am only an ant-hill. Make me a mountain.
I am only a feather. Make me a wing.
I am only a rag. Make me a king.

> — A prayer from Mexico

205. Surround Me, Lord

Be, Lord, within me to strengthen me,
without me to preserve, over me to shelter,

beneath to support, before me to direct,
behind me to bring back, round about me to fortify.

— LANCELOT ANDREWS

206. God Alone

Almighty God, give us wisdom to perceive you,
intellect to understand you,
diligence to seek you,
patience to wait for you,
eyes to behold you,
a heart to meditate upon you,
and life to proclaim you,
through the power of the Spirit of our Lord Jesus Christ.

— ST. BENEDICT OF NURSIA

207. Baptize Our Hearts

O Lord, baptize our hearts
into a sense of the conditions and needs of all men.

— GEORGE FOX

208. The Canticle of Brother Sun

O most high, almighty Lord God,
To you belong praise, glory, honor, and all blessings.

Praise to my Lord God with all his creatures,
And especially our brother the sun, who brings us the day
And who brings us the light;

Fair is he who shines with such great splendor;
O Lord, he signifies you to us!

Praise to my Lord our sister the moon and for the stars,
Which he has set clear and lovely in heaven.

Praise to my Lord for our brother the wind, for air and
  clouds, calms and all weather
By which you sustain life in all creatures.

Praise to my Lord for all who pardon one another for his
  love's sake,
And who endure weakness and tribulation;

Blessed are they who peaceably shall endure;
For you, O God, shall give them a crown!

Praise to my Lord for our sister, the death of the body
From which no man escapes.
Woe to him who dies in mortal sin!

Blessed are they who are found walking in your most holy
  will,
For the second death shall have no power to do them harm.

Praise and bless the Lord and give him thanks,
And serve him with great humility.

— ST. FRANCIS OF ASSISI

209. We Shall Lack No Good Thing

Almighty God,
who knowest our necessities before we ask,
and our ignorance in asking:
set free thy servants
from all anxious thoughts for the morrow;
give us contentment with thy good gifts;
and confirm our faith
that according as we seek thy kingdom,

thou wilt not suffer us to lack any good thing;
through Jesus Christ our Lord.

— St. Augustine

210. We Need Fear No Fall

He that is down needs fear no fall,
He that is low, no pride:
He that is humble ever shall
Have God to be his guide.

I am content with what I have,
Little be it or much:
And, Lord, contentment still I crave;
Because thou savest such.

— John Bunyan

211. Prayer for Understanding

Lord, help me not to despise or oppose
what I do not understand.

— William Penn

212. May Our Work Not Be a Burden

Lord, renew our spirits and draw our hearts unto thyself,
that our work may not be to us a burden, but a delight.
Oh, let us not serve thee
with the spirit of bondage as slaves,
but with the cheerfulness and gladness of children,
delighting ourselves in thee, and rejoicing in thy work.

— Benjamin Jenks

213. Make Me Slow to Anger

Father, make me quick to listen,
but slow to speak,
and slow to become angry.

—James 1:19

214. First Things First

God, let me put right before interest.
Let me put others before self.
Let me put the things of the spirit
before the things of the body.
Let me put the attainment of noble ends
above the enjoyment of present pleasures.
Let me put principle above reputation.
Let me put thee before all else.

—JOHN BAILLIE

215. Litany of Humility

O Jesus, meek and humble of heart, hear me.
From the desire of being esteemed,
   deliver me, Lord Jesus.
From the desire of being extolled, ...
From the desire of being honored, ...
From the desire of being praised, ...
From the desire of being preferred before others, ...
From the desire of being consulted, ...
From the desire of being approved, ...
From the desire of being highly regarded, ...
From the desire of being humiliated, ...
From the desire of being rebuked, ...
From the desire of being forgotten, ...

From the desire of being wronged, . . .
From the desire of being suspected, . . .

That others may be loved more than I,
   Jesus grant me the grace to desire it.
That in the opinion of the world, others may increase and
   I decrease, . . .
That others may be chosen and I passed over, . . .
That others be praised and I go unnoticed, . . .
That others should be preferred before me in everything, . . .
That others may become holier than I, provided that I may
   become as holy as I should. . . .

       — CARDINAL RAFAEL MERRY DEL VAL,
         secretary of state for Pope Pius X

216. Masters of Ourselves

O Lord, help us to be masters of ourselves
that we may be the servants of others.

       — SIR ALEXANDER HENRY PATERSON

217. Now Thank We All Our God

Now thank we all our God
with heart and hand and voices,
Who wondrous things hath done,
In whom his world rejoices;
who from our mothers' arms
Hath blessed us on our way
With countless gifts of love,
And still is ours today.

       — MARTIN RINKART

218. You're Obliged

Say not, merciful Virgin,
that you cannot help me;
for your beloved Son has given you
all power in heaven and on earth.
Say not that you ought not to assist me,
for you are the mother of all the poor children of Adam,
and mine in particular.

Since then, merciful Virgin,
you are my mother and are all-powerful,
what excuse can you offer
if you do not lend me your assistance?
See, my mother, see,
you are obliged to grant me what I ask,
and to yield to my entreaties. Amen.

— St. Francis de Sales

219. Right or Wrong

If I am right, thy Grace impart
Still in the right to stay:
If I am wrong, oh teach my heart
To find the better way.

— Alexander Pope

220. Strength for My Tasks

O Lord, I do not pray for tasks equal to my strength:
I ask for strength equal to my tasks.

— Phillips Brooks

221. Be at Peace, Then

Do not fear what may happen to you tomorrow.
The same Father who cares for you today,
will care for you tomorrow and every other day.
Either he will shield you from suffering
or he will give you unfailing strength to bear it.
Be at peace, then,
and put aside all anxious thoughts and imaginings.

— St. Francis de Sales

222. Keep Us From Falling

And now to him who is able to keep us from falling,
and lift us from the dark valley of despair
to the bright mountain of hope,
from the midnight of desperation
to the daybreak of joy;
to him be power and authority, forever and ever.

— Martin Luther King, Jr., a blessing spoken to his
congregation in Montgomery as he left them to devote
all his time to political action.

223. Let Us Be as Two Friends, Lord

It happens sometimes that the more we know our neighbor,
the less we love him,
but with you, O God, it is never so.
The more we know you the more we love you.
Knowledge of you kindles such a fire of love in our souls
that no room is left for other love or longing.

My Jesus, how good it is to love you!
Let me be like your disciples on Mt. Tabor,
seeing nothing else but you, my Savior.

Let us be as two friends,
neither of whom can bear to offend the other. Amen.

— St. John Vianney

224. You Are the Life of Things

Grandfather, Great Spirit,
once more behold me on earth
and learn to hear my feeble voice.
You lived first, and you are older than all need,
older than all prayer.
All things belong to you —
the two-legged, the four-legged,
the wings of the air, and all green things that live.

You have set the power
of the four quarters of the earth
to cross each other.
You have made me cross the good road,
the road of difficulties.
and where they cross the place is holy.
Day in, day out,
and forever more
you are the life of things.

— Black Elk

PART III

Original, Contemporary Prayers by and for Men

"Make me one with everything." This is the common prayer of our contemporaries. (And it's also the answer to the modern riddle: "What did the Zen student say to the hot dog vendor?")

Unity and connectedness are clearly the themes of so much of our prayer today in a culture where it's easy to become isolated, marginalized, disconnected. That's why in this section of *A Man's Guide to Prayer* you'll find prayers that seek connectedness and unity with family, creation, God. The feelings and the prayers are real for us modern men.

In reading a "how-to" article recently in a spirituality journal, I came upon some good advice worth sharing. "I used to write 'Prayer' on my calendar," wrote the author, "as a reminder to pray regularly. But before long it became so much of a 'technical obligation' for me that I gave up. Now I write 'God' on my calendar."

As you read through and select your favorite prayers from the following original contributions from contemporary men, let's together remember it's *God* we're after even more than *prayer*.

225. The Man's Prayer That Wasn't

_____
_____
_____

This is a test.
This is only a test.
In the event of an actual emergency,
The above might have been an actual prayer
that one of us guys might have prayed.
We now return you
to actual prayers.

226. Cowboy's Prayer

"Say your prayers!"
shouts the bad guy in black
as he pulls out his six-shooter.
"Dance!" says he
as he shoots at my feet.
Lord, why does it take
someone pointing a gun at me
to make me dance —
or say my prayers?

227. A Litany for the Modern Man Who Knows Himself All Too Well

From taking on the world by myself,
  Lord, preserve me.
From being too driven,
  Lord, preserve me.
From becoming a "control freak,"
  Lord, preserve me.
From being too withholding,
  Lord, preserve me.
From being too unemotional,
  Lord, preserve me.
From being "Mr. Right All the Time,"
  Lord, preserve me.
From isolating myself too much,
  Lord, preserve me.
From not doing the drudge work around the house,
  Lord, preserve me.
From being Mr. Tough Guy,
  Lord, preserve me.
From being too self-sufficient,
  Lord, preserve me.
From feeling that I always have to win,
  Lord, preserve me.
From being too proud,
  Lord, preserve me.
From not being a good listener,
  Lord, preserve me.
From never saying "I'm sorry,"
  Lord, preserve me.
From not giving myself permission to be weak once in a
  while,
  Lord, preserve me.

From caring more about sports than about relationships,
> Lord, preserve me.
From hiding my pain and my fears all the time,
> Lord, preserve me.
From "handling" things all the time instead of feeling them,
> Lord, preserve me.
From feeling like I have to be Superman,
> Lord, preserve me.
From being too: practical, productive, results-oriented,
industrious, efficient, impersonal, analytical, impersonal,
mechanical, focused, stubborn,
> Lord, preserve me.
From going it alone — without people, and without YOU,
> Lord, preserve me. Amen.

228. Transform Me, Lord

Father, you created me
to be Your living temple.
I open myself to your presence.
Come and live in me.
May Your Holy Spirit,
living and working in me,
transform me into the likeness
of Your beloved Son, Jesus.

—Eric Lies, O.S.B.

229. Husband's Prayer

Loving God,
help me always remember
what I said before you as my witness,
to my wife on our wedding day:

"I promise to be true to you . . .
in good times and in bad . . .
for richer and for poorer,
in sickness and in health,
until death do us part."
That was my promise,
for the sake of love.
I ask you for the sake of love
to give me the grace I need
to keep those promises
in big things and in small,
before children and after,
in youth and in old age,
when it's easy —
and when it's not. Amen.

230. The Little Boy's Hand

Give me a little hand, Lord,
the little hand of a boy,
a boy who trusts in the darkness,
a boy who reaches out
for a Father's hand to lead the sure way home.
Amen.

231. Prayer That My Suffering Mother May Die Peacefully

Lord, she needs to come to you.
Please, Lord, open your beautiful door to her
and show her to the couch
where Dad is watching Groucho Marx
and eating popcorn

and drinking a Pepsi
and laughing with Mom
and it's Saturday night again.
Amen.

232. A Failed Miracle

Jesus,
sometimes I wish there had been
just one failed miracle in your life,
in your story,
Where you would say, maybe,
"Lazarus, come forth,"
and nobody'd come forth.
I could relate to that.
But then again
on that black Friday afternoon,
I guess that was a pretty good failure,
with nobody coming forth.
I can relate to that.
Amen.

233. Rocket Man

Lord,
make me a rocket man.
Strip away from me
everything that ain't rocket,
every bit of extra weight
and cargo
and decoration.
Then make me soar,
me, the rocket man,
to you. Amen.

234. Prayer of the Grown Man

Lord, I used to pray for a pony;
now I pray for *no* pony, please!
I used to pray for super excitement;
now I pray for soup!
I used to pray that I'd catch the big one;
now I pray that someone else will catch it, clean it,
and deliver it to me cooked!
Amen.

235. More Serenity

Lord, God,
give me the peace
of not always having to know
what's going to happen next.
Amen.

236. Prayer of a Hu-Man

Dear God,
I know that as a man,
a hu-man,
I'm going to have to suffer in life;
and sometimes we have to suffer
if we want to live right.
It has to be that way.
You, God,
are gonna get us
and it's gonna hurt
before it doesn't anymore
and all is well, very well.
Amen.

237. Prayer to Keep Ambition in Check

Dear Jesus,
I remember that after one of your great miracles,
and after one of your great speeches,
the crowds closed in on you,
wanting to make you King.

"But Jesus went off to be alone."
Amen.

238. Businessman's Prayer

Lord,
Albert Einstein once wrote:
"I want to know God's thoughts;
all the rest are details."
Lord, as my desk gets covered with details,
and my briefcase gets filled with details,
and my calendar gets filled with details,
and my budget gets filled with details,
and my meetings get filled with details...
please give me your thoughts.
Amen.

239. A Father's Prayer While Vacationing with Family in a Cabin in the Woods

Lord, thank you
for bringing us to this holy place.
Here we laugh and play and hike and rest;
here we build family.
Here we find quiet and space,
freedom and food,

sun and rain,
laughter and love.
Here I say thank you, God,
for this my life. Amen.

240. Prayer of a Man during Sickness

I'm not used to this, God,
me being taken care of,
me being weak and flat on my back.
And I don't like it one bit.
Get me out of here, God.
Give me back my strength and health, I pray,
and I'll try not to take them so for granted again.
Amen.

241. A Brother's Prayer

"Let there be no strife,
for all men are brothers,"
wrote St. Benedict.
Fifteen hundred years ago
it was no easier to be a brother
than it is now, Lord,
a real brother.
Why is it, Lord, that sometimes it's easier
being a brother to a stranger
than to your own brother or sister?
Today I ask you, God,
to bless my brothers and sisters
and I ask you to forgive me for the times
I was not a brother to my own brothers and sisters,
much less to my brothers and sisters
in the "extended family" in which you placed me.

Teach me, Lord, let it sink in,
that since you are our loving Parent,
we are truly all your sons and daughters
and that means we're all stuck in this thing together.
Amen.

242. Prayer of a Father Waiting in the Coliseum Parking Lot While His Teenage Daughter Is Inside at a Rock Concert

Dear God, the music plays on tonight,
on and on,
and it's so loud I can hear it out here
in the parking lot.
As I patiently wait here for the concert to end
after just one more encore! — I hope —
I pray that my daughter
and her community of young people
feel the positive power of music.
May it lift them up and inspire them
as it has done in so many years past.
And, Lord, remind me that a little loudness
and some occasional wildness
will not in themselves put this generation
on the path to ruin and damnation!
They, like us, must march to the drums of their time —
just as we did.
Their paths must meander — and even veer widely —
so widely sometimes that they are totally out of our sight,
and out of our control.
Bless my little girl, God, and bring her out here soon —
and bring us all to *your* great sell-out concert
someday. Amen.

243. Solitary Man

Loving God,
I come before you wifeless, childless,
but not care-less nor care-free.
Renew in me the compassion for my fellow human beings
that you exhibit in your loving care for all creation,
and show to me that same care and kindness
to accompany me all my days. Amen.

244. Help Me Fling My Life into the Darkness

May I follow a life of compassion
in pity for the suffering of all living things.
Teach me to live with reverence for life everywhere,
to treat life as sacred and respect all that breathes.
O Father, I grope amid the shadows of doubt and fear,
but I long to advance toward the light.
Help me to fling my life like a flaming firebrand
into the gathering darkness of the world.

—Dr. Albert Schweitzer

245. Prayer of the Widower

Lord, now you know why
I loved my wife with all my life,
and do forever more.
She's with you now, Lord, at home,
and you see her
at her gentle, kind, and loving best.
Keep me company, too, Lord,
as I wait here below till the happily ever after.
Amen.

246. Prayer for the Kids

Strengthen them, O Lord,
And keep them from the strangers' ways.

> —SHELDON HARNICK, Sabbath Prayer
> from "Fiddler on the Roof"

247. Metanoia

I met a noia
On the way
To looking for
A way to pray.
I asked the noia
What to do.
Let God be God
The noia said,
Before you're dead
He'll meta you!

248. Prayer for Purity

Take my body, Jesus,
eyes and ears and hands.
Never let them, Jesus,
help to do thee wrong.

Take my heart and fill it
full of love for thee.
All I have I give thee
and give thyself to me.

> — "Learned at a high school retreat, sixty-five years ago,"
> says my friend Benedictine monk ERIC LIES

249. Thomas Merton Prayer

My Lord God, I have no idea where I am going.
I do not see the road ahead of me.
I cannot know for certain where it will end.
Nor do I really know myself,
and the fact that I think I am following your will
does not mean that I am actually doing so.
But I believe that the desire to please you
does in fact please you.
And I hope I have that desire in all that I am doing.
I hope that I will never do anything apart from that desire.
And I know that if I do this
you will lead me by the right road
though I may know nothing about it.
Therefore will I trust you always
though I may seem to be lost and in the shadow of death.
I will not fear, for you are ever with me,
and you will never leave me to face my perils alone.

— THOMAS MERTON, *Thoughts in Solitude,*
© Abbey of Gethsemani

250. Conversion Prayer

Thank You, Lord, for this, my life!

— TOM HANKS, "Joe" in the movie *Joe Versus the Volcano*

251. HOLY.DOT.COM!
Computer Password Prayers

"I use the computer a lot in my work," writes Tom Ballard, *Newburgh, Indiana, "since I am a software engineer. For my passwords onto various computers and into various accounts I*

always use short 'prayers' of sorts, such as 'HOLYHOLY.' This
way I feel like my work is a prayer, too, and I am praying all
day long."

> HOLYHOLY
> SACREDHEART
> ALLELUIA
> GODISLOVE

252. The Prayer of the Poet

And once again
mysteriously
you hear me when I call —
you answer.
Where I least expect,
where, in fact, I fled you,
not knowing that I did.
And my mercenary pen
records your mercy.

— MURRAY BODO, O.F.M.

253. Dear God, I'm a Dad

Let me show my family
the "strong stuff"
you made me for:
steady guidance,
firm hugs,
solid support,
concrete advice,
lasting love. Amen.

— Abbey Press poster

254. Prayer Inspired by Kentucky Poet Wendell Berry

Here, Lord, is where we do
what we are going to do —
the only chance we got.
Help us dig in
and do it well.

255. Recessional

God of our fathers, known of old,
Lord of our far-flung battle-line,
Beneath whose awful Hand we hold
Dominion over palm and pine —
Lord God of Hosts, be with us yet,
Lest we forget — lest we forget!

— RUDYARD KIPLING

256. Teach Me to Live the Jesus Way

Jesus, teach me
to pray like you prayed,
to act like you acted,
to decide like you decided
to live the Jesus Way:
to live like you,
to die like you
to rise like you. Amen.

257. Letting Go of Control

God's will,
nothing more,

nothing less,
nothing else.

> — From a man on retreat at the Abbey of Gethsemani,
> Trappist, Kentucky

258. The Force

May the Force be with you.

> — *Star Wars*

259. Prayer of a Promise-Keeper

Dear God,
before you and before your people,
I made some promises, Lord.
Help me to always
look to my commitments
and look to you, my Lord,
to help me keep them.
I pray to be a man of my word
and a man of your Word.
Amen.

260. Rinky-Dink Prayers

"Just being aware of God is not enough," writes my friend David Knight. "We need to interact with God as we do with a friend. And we can do this in a number of ways, on a number of different levels."

One way is to make constant use of "rinky-dink" prayer. A rinky-dink prayer is a prayer for something that is not important enough to bother the Almighty about. When we make it, we become conscious that God is our friend.

I discovered rinky-dink prayer one evening when I was putting a roof on a carport. I was pressing to get finished before dark, and in my haste I kept dropping roofing tacks onto the driveway, where I knew they would lie waiting for my car tires. I noticed that each time I dropped a tack and scrambled down the ladder in the increasing darkness to look for it, I would start to say a prayer: "Lord, help me find that tack!"

And it irked me. My spontaneous reaction to making the prayer was irritation. I felt humiliated, degraded in some way because I was asking God for help to do what I was perfectly capable of doing myself. In an attempt to justify my irritation, I told myself, "If my best friend was president of the United States I wouldn't call him to fix a parking ticket." And then the thought came to me, "No, but if my best friend were standing at the bottom of the ladder, the first thing I would do when I dropped a tack would be to yell down, "Hey, did you see where that tack went?"

So now I pray to him constantly, asking God to do anything I'd ask a friend to do: "Lord, help me find a parking place." "Show me a good restaurant." "Don't let me blow it on this phone call." "Lord, keep the light green till I get through."

261. I'm Not Superman

Dear God,
I know I'm not Superman.
It's pretty clear to me
most every time I try to rescue the day for someone
in my family or at my job...
or work on that darned garage door or crazy computer.
And, yet, I know, great God,
you made us all super,

with hearts and minds that can glimpse, every day,
the supernatural.
Thank you, Lord. Amen.

262. Fifty Times I Thank You – A Litany of Thanksgiving on My Fiftieth Birthday

Thank you, God, for thunderstorms • my hammock • kick
the tin can • coaching soccer • Bobby Kennedy • zinnias
• Mozart • the Mikado • our first TV in 1954 • church
picnics • hayrides • my mail-order mechanical calculator •
the heat register at the bottom of the stairs in the old farm-
house • big Christmas trees • little kids, especially mine •
Professor Irwin Corey • Joe Morgan with a big lead off of
first • the pony at my Uncle Ted's • swimming pools at mo-
tel weekends with family • Mom's sugar cookies • listening
to Mom and Dad talk in the car while us kids were in the
back seat • mail call in the seminary • Annie Dillard •
Stephen Jay Gould • "Moon River" • quiet • my bee-bee
gun • wisteria • the family drive-in theater • the smell of
blown-out church candles • riding a bike after not riding a
bike for twenty-five years • ping pong • Demerol for kidney
stones • the 1975 World Series • pitch and catch • college
nights • tulips • seeing the *Ten Commandments* in 1957 •
Perry Como • naps • coffee • Click and Clack • The Barn
• fireplaces • Indiana Jones • Mom and Dad and Sisters
and Brother • my great job • rhubarb pie • *The Hobbit* •
wife Mikie's bridge over my troubled waters. Amen.

263. Then, Lord, I'll Know

Whenever I'm in doubt, Lord,
or when the world becomes too much with me,

and my self becomes even more,
teach me this good expedient:
to recall the face of the poorest
and most helpless person I've ever seen —
and ask myself if what I contemplate
will be of any use to that person.
Then, Lord, I know,
I will see my own troubled world
and my own troubled self melt away.

> — Inspired by a saying of Gandhi

264. Thank You

"Thanks, God."

> — After MEISTER ECKHART, who is quoted as saying:
> "If the only prayer you ever say in your entire life
> is thank you, it will be enough."

265. I Adore You

O God!
If I adore you out of fear of Hell,
burn me in Hell!
If I adore you out of desire for
Paradise, lock me out of Paradise.
But if I adore you for yourself alone,
do not deny me to your eternal beauty.

> — Rabi'a

266. Count Me In, Lord

Oh, when the saints go marchin' in,
Oh, when the saints go marchin' in,

I wanna be, Lord, in that number,
When the saints go marchin' in.

—Made famous in song by LOUIS ARMSTRONG

267. Prayers of the "Express Male"

Lord, teach me that
I don't have to
...do it all
...by myself
...right now.
Amen.

268. Gandhi's Prayer

I will be truthful.
I will suffer no injustice.
I will be free from fear.
I will not use force.
I will be of good will to all men.

—MAHATMA GANDHI

269. This Guy's Prayer

You see
this guy?
This guy's in love with you.
Yes, Lord, this guy.
Who looks at you
the way I do?
It's swell,
I can tell:

We know each other
very well.
Please say you're in love with
This guy.
If not I'll just die.

— Adapted from and inspired by
a BURT BACHARACH love song

270. Prayer of the Divorced Man

It feels like failure, God,
and I guess that's what it is.
And yet it's so much more than failure,
and so much less.
Give me a new starting point, Lord,
new hope, new direction, new light.
This failure feeling is getting old.
Amen.

271. The Logic Prayer – after Rabbi Harold S. Kushner

Lord, God, if we men
be too logical, too rational, too smart,
and if this logic, this reason, this wisdom
tells us you aren't there . . .
or you don't care —
Don't let us give up on *you;*
let us give up on logic
and reason
and wisdom itself.
Amen.

272. Prayer of a Father

Lord,
I know that a dad is someone
who loves his children no matter what,
someone who lifts them up,
and leads them on the right path,
and lets them go — at just the right moment.
Teach me to be a dad
who shares his faith in simple, ordinary ways,
someone who encourages his children
and believes in them throughout their lives,
someone who hears with his heart,
leads with his life,
and loves forever. Amen.

— Adapted from an Abbey Press text

273. Yes!

Night is drawing nigh.
For all that has been —
Thanks!
For all that shall be —
Yes!

— DAG HAMMARSKJÖLD

274. Saved from Doom

Lord, we survive — thanks to you:
the delivery from the womb,
the tests in the classroom,
the challenges of the bridegroom,
the pressures of the boardroom,
... and the permanence of the tomb.

275. Me and You, God

Me and you, God.
Me and you.
But mostly you.

— Prayer of a man carrying a heavy weight

276. A Muslim Meal Prayer

In the name of God, most gracious and most merciful.

— Translated from Arabic

277. Dependence Day Prayer

Dear Lord,
today I declare my
Dependence (on You) Day!

278. Prayer for Starting Over

Dear God, give me the courage to begin again —
to overlook the difficulties,
to overcome the obstacles,
and to stay open to the moment as best I can.
Help me be patient enough
to know it takes time to start over,
and wise enough to ask for help
from friends and family when I need it.
As I look to the future,
may I reflect on the past
and remember the lessons it's taught me.
And, God, may I always look to you
for strength and guidance.
Amen.

279. Prayer of the Data-Gatherer

Lord, help me remember
this simple commandment you gave my heart:
Thou shalt not live by information alone. Amen.

280. Prayer for Serenity

God, grant me serenity
to accept the things I cannot change,
courage to change the things I can,
and wisdom to know the difference:
living one day at a time:
accepting hardship as a pathway to peace:
taking, as Jesus did, this sinful world as it is,
not as I would have it:
trusting that You will make all things right
if I surrender to your will:
so that I may be reasonably happy in this life
and supremely happy with You forever in the next. Amen.

—REINHOLD NIEBUHR

281. Give Me Your Orders

Holy Spirit,
Soul of my soul, I adore You.
Enlighten me, guide me,
strengthen me, console me.
Tell me what I should do,
give me Your orders.
I promise to do whatever
you ask me to do
and to accept whatever
You permit to happen to me.

Only let me know Your will.
Amen.

— CARDINAL MERCIER

282. Abba ... Father ... Daddy

Tell me a story, Abba, Father, Daddy;
sit me on your lap.
Make it *our* story,
Abba, Father, Daddy;
make us run and jump and clap.
When we get ourselves in trouble
at least we'll be together.
And make the story end with
happy happy forever.
Amen.

283. All the Way Home

What have I been waiting for?
I know very well mystic Julian's prayer about
"and all will be well, and all will be well,
and all will be very, very well,"
but now I want to pray,
"and all *is* well and all *is* well
and all is very, very well."
What makes it so?
The company I keep
and the Company I keep.
Walk with me, Lord,
all the way home.
Amen.

284. We Can Handle It

O God,
keep me mindful of yesterday,
but don't let me live there only.
"Today has enough cares of its own," as Jesus taught.
Help me to remember the times
I thought I was all alone
and suddenly found you there alongside me.
Help me, too,
to know whatever it is back there
behind me on the trail —
even if it's "gaining on me" —
that we can handle it together
if it should catch up with us.
Amen.

285. Prayer for Courage

Lord, may I have the courage
to embrace each day,
to stand for what's right
to dare to be myself,
to risk the unknown,
to challenge the accepted,
to let go when I must,
to place my future into your hands.
Amen.

286. I Accept in All Gratitude

In Thy fullness my Lord, filled with Thy Grace,
for the purpose of union with Thee
and to satisfy and glorify Thy Creation;

with thanks to Thee with all my heart,
with all my love for Thee,
with all adoration for Thy Blessings,
I accept Thy gifts as they have come to me;
this [food, day, family] is Thy blessing —
and in Thy service I accept in all gratitude my Lord.
Amen.

— MAHARISHI MAHESH YOGI

287. Surrender

I can't.
You must.
I'm yours.
Show me the way.

— From the movie *Romero*

288. Beginning Again and Again

God, You are the beginning and the end.
Help me to realize that I am in a new beginning.
Oh, how treacherous new beginnings can be!
Grant me the grace not to agonize
so much as to simply collapse and say, "I give up."
For You are the true spring of life and meaning.
You are the One Who holds me up.
Allow me to see that with time
this, as all beginnings do, will take shape.
Do not let me get stuck in the clutches of my inner critic
where I leave little or no room
for Your new beginnings in my life.
Rather, grace me with an openness
to stand before You in grateful receptivity.

I praise You for allowing me to begin again ...
and again ... and again.
I ask this through Jesus Christ your Son,
who lives and reigns with You and the Holy Spirit,
One God forever and ever. Amen.

— ANDY GARNER

289. Prayer for a Young Boy's Heart

Lord, give me the happy heart of a young boy,
the young boy I once was
who delighted in that old $3.00 red bicycle
and my fourteen-year-old sister's transistor radio.
Give me that boyish heart again
that found such joy in catching small fish
in a small pond,
and drinking big bottles of Coke
and eating big bowls of popcorn
with big brother and big sister ...
and little sister, too.
Give me the happy heart of the young boy
who wanted to make every hair on my head
a prayer of praise to you,
and who now, making the same prayer,
offers less prayer
But just as fervent, O Lord. Amen.

290. Black Is Beautiful, Man

O God, black is beautiful!
Let us be aware of black blessings:
Blessed be the black night that nurtures dreams.

Blessed be the black cave of imagination that births
   creativity.
Blessed be dark wombs that cradle us.
Blessed be black loam that feeds our bodies.
Blessed be black jazz that nourishes our souls.
Blessed be black energy that swirls into gracefulness.
Blessed be black coal that heats us.
Blessed be black boiling clouds hurling down lightning and
   cleansing rain.
Blessed be even our own darkness, our raw undeveloped
   cave of shadows.
O God, when we befriend black and do not deny its power,
Black is beautiful indeed!
May we discover blessings within our holy dark!

> — WILLIAM FITZGERALD, in *Praying,*
> November–December 1997

291. Not a Martyr

Teach me, O God, not to torture myself,
Not to make a martyr out of myself,
Through stifling reflection,
But rather teach me to breathe deeply in faith.

> — SØREN KIERKEGAARD

292. A Prayer That Can't Be Answered – Unless It's Prayed

Dear Lord, I know that . . .
life without a purpose is barren indeed;
there can't be a harvest unless there's a seed.
There can't be attainment unless there's a goal,
and man's but a robot unless he's got soul.

If we send out no ships, no ships can come in,
and unless there's a contest nobody can win.
For games can't be won unless they are played,
and prayers can't be answered ... unless they are prayed!

—Adapted from a verse by HELEN STEINER RICE

293. A Prayer That Goes Two Ways

Be with me.

294. Prayer of a Grieving Man

Lord, I know now that the journey from grief to healing
is neither simple nor direct.
There are side trips, detours, wrong turns.
I pray only that I be on a meandering river
which knows the way home.
And I pray you stay with me.
Teach me as my dark night ends
that my grief places me in good company —
in the company of my human family — and with you.
At the dawning of the new day,
I pray that I may stand arm-in-arm with all creation —
as your Eternal Light breaks forth once again.
Amen.

295. Real Presence – A Parent's Prayer

Let my heart be a wide and welcome harbor
where my children come to rest.
May these arms stretch wide and strong
to hold his fear, her hurt,
their tattered sense of self.

May there be a solidness within me
on which their pain may crash and recede
and I remain.

Let my presence be an island to them
in storm-tossed seasons,
rising up from troubled waters
to offer shelter, respite, and firm dry ground.

May they find me
a haven to send battered souls
until the day the certainty of such solid ground
launches them to sail
uncharted waters unafraid.

— TOM McGRATH

296. Prayer of the Big Game Hunter

Lord, it is thee I seek;
do thou find me. Amen.

297. What Would You Do, Lord?

Lord, throughout this day,
as I try to follow You,
let this be my rule to live by:
What would Jesus do?
When a friend or loved one
asks me for a moment or two,
may I think of one thing only:
What would Jesus do?
In all my dealings, help me
to be honest, fair, and true,
to measure each decision by:

What would Jesus do?
When I am feeling troubled
and I turn in prayer to You,
give me the reason to decide:
What would Jesus do?
Then when the day is ended,
may I resolve anew
to guide tomorrow by the motto:
What would Jesus do?
Amen.

298. Dad, Praying for Little Jackie

I tuck my little girl into bed and we say our prayers. "Hail Mary, full of grace. God bless...." And then I make a cross on her forehead and I whisper to God, "Please, God, help Jackie learn how to speak. Help her to grow up and live a good, happy life. Take away her autism."

As I leave the room I am completely bifurcated by this last prayer. Part of me is ashamed of asking this of God. How presumptuous of me to think that I can outguess the will of the Creator of the universe.

How dare I question His wisdom? Jackie was born with autism for a purpose. This is not a random act of cruelty. There is something to be gained here, something to be learned. After all, isn't Jackie the source of great laughter in my life? To watch her dance across the room, singing her truncated version of a favorite song, is sheer beauty. To hear her say "Wizzabah" instead of "Wizard of Oz" is delightful. How often do I and Jimmy and Jo Ann imitate her because her verbal mannerisms are so irresistible?

The other part of me is less passive. Didn't Jesus tell us that if we had faith the size of a grain of mustard seed we could tell the mountain to move and it would cast itself into the sea? Isn't that the essence of prayer? Is it, then, the lack of faith on my part which prevents me from healing my little girl? Do I rage at myself for lack of faith, or do I blame God for not listening?

I am not good at praying. I feel awkward and vaguely ashamed, as if I were asking someone for a loan. But I know that this is not what God wants of me. I try to make prayer casual sometimes, like an off-the-cuff chat with a good friend. But that's not it, either. I want my prayers to be as effortless and simple as those of Jimmy when he was first learning to speak. He would God bless everything that came into his mind — from relatives to hamburgers to French fries.

I want to pray constantly, to have thoughts of God so grounded in my being that to move would be to pray. I want my thoughts to be pure white light. And I want Jackie to sit down and talk about all of this with me.

— THOMAS KALB

299. A Motorist's Prayer – for Men

Grant steady hand and watchful eye,
that none be hurt as I pass by.
Guide my wheels along the way,
increase my vision night and day.
Make me humble no matter the cost,
and ask directions when I'm lost!
Amen.

300. Why Am I Here, God?

Why am I here, God,
and what should I do?

Bloom where I'm planted
or seek a new view?
I sometimes feel useless,
just filling up days.
You got something in mind,
can you clear up this haze?
I know there's a reason,
I know I've got worth.
Please send the directions
Attention: Me, Earth.
Amen.

301. Not Just a Little

Dear God,
teach me that
to be saved doesn't mean
 ... being just a little encouraged
 ... being just a little comforted
 ... being just a little relieved.
Teach me that it means
being pulled out like a log
from a burning fire.
Amen.

— Inspired by KARL BARTH

302. Prayer for Courage

When tensions build up on the job
and pressures at home begin to mount
and life becomes almost too much to bear,
I sometimes get scared, Lord.
I get the urge to run away and hide

like the young man in the garden who fled
when the police came to arrest You, Jesus.
How is it that you stood your ground
and did not back off from your teaching?
A little while before,
You sweated blood,
but you found strength to yield
to the Father's will
and draw power from it.
The next time I waver
or grow faint-hearted,
help me to stand firm,
and, having found the source of strength,
to reach out to others
who may be just as scared as I.
Amen.

— LEONARD FOLEY, O.F.M.

303. Another Prayer That Goes Two Ways

I am here for you.

304. A Police Officer's Prayer

Help me, Lord, to be
a good and capable police officer.
Give me the courage to face the unknown
and to act on my convictions.
Give me the wisdom to remain above the temptations
and frustrations I will meet.
Give me the dedication to do the best job I can.

— From an Abbey Press plaque

305. Prayer of a Brand New Father

Lord, I'm walking,
but my feet aren't touching the ground!
Imagine that! Me a dad!
God, the joy and the suffering
all together wound in one here in childbirth.
Thank you, God, for our new little baby,
thank you thank you thank you!

306. Prayer of the Computer Operator

Guide my keystrokes,
keep my programs alive,
protect me from viruses
and back up my drive. Amen.

— Abbey Press "mousepad" text

307. Prayer of a Man for a Childlike Heart

Dear God,
I come to you as a child to a loving parent,
asking you to help me.
I know no valley is so deep,
no room so dark,
that you are not in them with me.
May I rest assured
in your goodness and love.
May I sleep in peace,
knowing you are awake.
And may I let go
of foolish worries,
knowing you are holding me close
all the time. Amen.

308. Big Hands

Lord, you gave me big hands
to hold,
to guide,
to build,
to support,
to give,
to touch.
And for all of this I give you
a big hand. Amen.

309. A Firefighter's Prayer

Lord, help me to be a good and dedicated firefighter.
Give me the strength to face the boredom
as well as the fear.
Give me the wisdom
to make quick decisions
and compassionate choices.
Give me the courage
to bear the responsibilities
and duties of doing my job well.

310. A Man's Prayer for Help

Dear God, help me be courageous;
I'm tired of being just "strong"!
Help me reach inside — and out —
to get the help you offer me.
It's hard to stand up, alone,
to everything the world
throws at me.
So help me

not waste my energy
when I'm already down and out
on "being strong" and "taking it like a man."
Instead, help me be courageous. Amen.

311. Prayer of a Grown Man Who Has Lost His Parents

Dear Lord,
sometimes I just wish
I could be
someone's son
again. Amen.

— WALTER SPIERDOWIS

312. Prayer for Humility

Lord, I know that sometimes
you leave in us some defects of character —
so that we can learn humility.
For without these defects,
we would immediately soar above the clouds
in our own estimation —
and would place our throne there instead of yours.
Protect us, Lord, from such perdition.

— Paraphrase of prayer of THEOPHANE THE RECLUSE,
early Christian Egyptian Desert Father

313. Why God – Again?

Why God — again?
You can't be that cruel!

— Prayer of despair of Olympic speed skater whose hand
scraped the ice causing him to lose the 500-meter race

314. And Yet Again — Why?

God, sometimes I wonder why you do the things you do.

— Prayer of professional boxer whose sharp right blow
caused a fatal cerebral hemorrhage of his opponent

315. Ultimate Prayer of Surrender

Lord, I can't.
You can.
I'll let you.
Amen.

316. A Sportsman's Prayer (with a bit of tongue in cheek)

Almighty Creator,
without your permission
not a hair falls from a head,
nor a sparrow to the ground.
Grant, I beseech you,
that each [field goal, free throw, serve, etc.]
of my team
be guided and directed by your ordinance,
and may our opponents
not be praying as ardently as we!
Amen.

317. A Farmer's Prayer

I plant the seed,
You make it grow.
You send the rain,
I work the hoe.

318. Another Prayer That Goes Two Ways

Stay with me.

319. A Son's Prayer at His Mother's Death

Lord, my mom died today,
and I don't know how to feel.
I thought it might be better than this;
she suffered so much.
Her ravaged body
made it hard to even look at her
and not feel very, very sad
at the price some innocents
must pay to get admitted to the better world.
Lord, on Friday I was with her and told her
what a good mom she's been.
"I miss my mom," said she.
"She was a good mom."
We got Mom a white Rosary for Christmas,
just two weeks ago.
As soon as she saw it, she kissed the crucifix.
Jesus,
it's your turn to kiss and hold her now.
This is my prayer, Lord:
No more "terrors of the night," Lord.
Not for Mom.
No more.
Never.
Amen.
Alleluia!

320. A Grandfather's Prayer

Lord, help me be:

G — Generous and caring.
R — Respectful of all.
A — Affectionate!
N — Never-ending in my kindness.
D — Devoted to family.
P — Patient as a grandmother!
A — Always grateful to be a grandpa.

321. A Father's Day Prayer

Lord, I pray, to the Father up above,
asking you to bless me with your guidance and your love.
I don't pray for worldly wealth but ask you to impart
wisdom and contentment, peace of mind and heart.
I ask the Lord to grant me, too, the deep serenity,
of sharing simple pleasures with friends and family.
Most of all, I pray I know the great effect I have,
on all the lives around me — just by being Dad!

— Adapted from an Abbey Press prayer print

322. A Godfather's Prayer

Lord, may I make you an offer you can't refuse?
I will live in love for you. Amen.

323. Prayer of a Man on a Spiritual Retreat

Dear God,
it's Saturday night and I'm here
at the Abbey of Gethsemani,

where you can hear yourself *not* think!
I'm dead in the center of a big Kentucky rain.
A good, cleansing rain.
And it's washing some things away from me, I pray:
layer after layer of the disguises I wear
out there
but not here:
First to wash away is the Rich Businessman thing,
the successful exec,
then the world-famous writer,
editor,
and the rescuer of the distressed.
And there goes the perfect husband and father,
and next the *pretty*-good husband and father.

What's left, Lord,
after the rain?
Well, it's still raining,
but we're down to a guy
who just wants to look in the mirror
and see
what You want to see.
Amen.

324. Prayer for My Dad on the Day of His Burial

Today, O God,
we are burying a farmer,
a man who embraced the earth,
for over forty years putting things into the ground
and never once knowing for sure
what would come out.
Today, Lord,
we are planting

what no power on earth
can keep in the ground.
It's only June
and the corn is ten feet high.
Amen.

325. Time and Material –
A Construction Worker's Prayer

Lord, give me the skills
and the tools
to build your kingdom:
Let me not build up walls
between people
or to block folks out,
but to house them and hold them
to do your good.
Let me build roads and bridges
that cross over and connect
the people in your care.
Let me raise roofs that shelter
your people from the storm —
but not hide us from your loving face.
Give me strength, precision,
time and material, Lord,
and your helping hand. Amen.

326. An Environmentalist's Prayer

Dear God, I thank you
that they can't chop down clouds.
Amen.

— Inspired by a quip by HENRY DAVID THOREAU

327. Native American Husband and Father's Prayer

Great Spirit,
help us to know that
only for a short time
have you loaned us
to each other.

328. I'm Sorry

Ever-merciful, ever-forgiving God,
saying "I'm sorry" isn't easy for some of us guys.
It's hard to say to a family member, a friend, a co-worker;
it's even hard to say to you, Lord.
But . . . here goes:
I'm sorry. Amen.

329. Prayer to Ease Stress

Sometimes the stress I feel, Lord,
seems more than I can bear.
That's why I'm counting on you
because I know how much you care.
I know that troubles can teach,
so I'm not asking that they cease.
What I really need
is just a little bit of your peace.
Amen.

330. Prayer to Use Faith — as a Tool

Dear God, give me a faith that says
life is not "a tale told by an idiot."

Give me, God, a faith
that is from the heart — and is useful —
and is used and not forgotten
or chucked or left on the shelf
the first time life gets smashed up
or broken or shattered.
Amen.

331. Mechanic's Prayer

Lord, as I check the gauges,
adjust these belts,
grease these joints,
change these batteries,
help me remember
my own gauges and belts,
my own joints and batteries
need tune-ups and recharges, too.
Help me keep things
maintained and in balance,
by following the tips
in your Owner's Manual.
Amen.

332. Prayer of an Old Monk

Lord, I know that you love me.
And so I don't care what you do to me. Amen.

333. Superpower Prayer

Almighty and superpowerful God,
help me to remember that
when I work so hard to look and act

like a superpower myself,
I can end up looking pretty
superpowerless.
Amen.

334. A Final Prayer That Goes Two Ways

Thank you. I love you.

Acknowledgements and Bibliography

Thanks to all who have granted permission to include their prayers in this book. Thanks especially to Abbey Press for a goodly number of the prayers in this book, some of which have been slightly adapted. Thanks also to the monks of Saint Meinrad Archabbey who kindly offered their favorite prayers, as did a great many friends near and far, some of whom are named herein and some of whom are not. God bless you one and all! Amen.

Recommended Sources

Archibald, Chrestina Mitchell. *Say Amen: The African American Family's Book of Prayers.* New York: Dutton, 1997.

The Complete Book of Christian Prayer. New York: Continuum, 1996.

Couser, Thomas. *Real Men Pray: Prayer Thoughts for Husbands and Fathers.* St. Louis: Concordia, 1997.

Dollen, Charles, ed. *Prayer Book of the Saints.* Huntington, Ind.: Our Sunday Visitor, 1984.

The Doubleday Prayer Collection. Comp. Mary Batchelor. New York: Doubleday, 1996.

Dunn, Philip. *Prayer: Language of the Soul.* New York: Rodale, 1997.

Getz, Gene A. *The Measure of a Man: Attributes of a Godly Man.* Ventura, Calif.: Regal Books, 1974.

Hampton Wright, Vinita. *Prayers across the Centuries.* Wheaton, Ill.: Harold Shaw Publishers, 1993.

Parrinder, Geoffrey. *A Dictionary of Religious and Spiritual Quotations.* New York: Simon and Schuster, 1989.

Pollock, Constance and Daniel, eds. *The Book of Uncommon Prayer.* Dallas: Word Publishing, 1996.

PrayerNotes. Abbey Press, St. Meinrad, IN 47577.

Praying Magazine, NCR Publishing, Box 419335, Kansas City, MO 64141.

Roberts, Elizabeth, and Elias Amidon, eds. *Earth Prayers from Around the World,* San Francisco: HarperSanFrancisco, 1991.

———. *Life Prayers.* San Francisco: HarperSanFrancisco, 1996.

Schiller, David, ed. *The Little Book of Prayers.* New York: Workman, 1996.

Thompson, Keith, ed. *To Be a Man: In Search of the Deep Masculine.* New York: Putnam's, 1991

Subject Index

Index references are to prayer numbers

About the author: Linus Mundy's books include *Slow-down Therapy, The Complete Guide to Prayer-Walking, Grief Therapy for Men,* and *Seeking God Alone — and Together: A Retreat with Benedict and Bernard.* He is also founder of One Caring Place and is publisher of CareNotes. He serves as husband and father — and as publisher at Abbey Press in St. Meinrad, Indiana.

ALSO BY

Linus Mundy

■

The Complete Guide to Prayer-Walking
A Simple Path to Body-and-Soul Fitness

"Simply put, it's taking 'a stroll with your soul,' a simple, natural
method for growing spiritually as you're growing physically,"
says Linus Mundy, author of *Prayer-Walking*. 'Jesus did it.
Gandhi did it. A lot of holy people have done it.'
But it fits perfectly into today's frenzied times."
— *USA Today*

0-8245-1546-3; $13.95

■

Please support your local bookstore, or call 1-800-395-0690.
For a free catalog, please write us at
The Crossroad Publishing Company
370 Lexington Avenue, New York, NY 10017

We hope you enjoyed
A Man's Guide to Prayer.
Thank you for reading it.

crossroad